PILOT

For foreign and subsidiary rights, contact the author.

Cover design by Joe De Leon

ISBN: 978-1-954089-61-7   1 2 3 4 5 6 7 8 9 10

Printed in the United States of America

PILOT

PREPARING INTEGRAL LEADERS OF TOMORROW

NICHOLAS JOHN

INSPIRE

FOREWORD

You never know!

You never know when a seemingly chance encounter will create a lifelong friendship. Such is the case of my relationship with Nicholas John, the author of this book.

I was guest speaking for Bishop D. A. Lazarus at a leadership conference in Johannesburg, South Africa. In the audience was Nicholas. And it happened! As you will read in **PILOT**, God had and continues to have plans for us of Indian descent, born in different countries and at different times in history—yet, with the same passion. That of investing our lives into other leaders.

Google the word "leadership," and you'll receive over 2.5 billion responses. Many of them are definitions of leadership. Nicholas and I have a very simple one-word definition of leadership: *Others*.

That is why Nicholas has so appropriately named this book **PILOT**: *Preparing Integral Leaders Of Tomorrow*. You will hear Nicholas say that he is dedicating his life to the one endeavor of pouring himself into *others*, so leaders presently and in the future will lead and do so with integrity.

What are the qualities of an integral leader? Here are a few for you to consider as you prepare to read.

- Humble—This is the prerequisite to learning and growing. Arrogant people know it all.
- Self-aware—This is the prerequisite to knowing your possibilities and unique calling.
- God-aware—This is the prerequisite to knowing that you have been placed on this planet with a purpose.
- Community—This is the prerequisite to living a life of accountability.
- Selfless—This is the prerequisite to always keeping your life's focus on others.

I must admit that I was embarrassed when I read Nicholas's words because of the number of times I have been mentioned with such extravagant commendation. However, it hit me again. It hit me that we don't live casual lives. That our lives are consequential. That meeting someone could be a life changer for that person and you.

I wonder what would have happened if I had never met Nicholas John or we hadn't pursued our relationship—it would have definitely been my loss.

You are not about to read a book. You're about to meet Nicholas John.

He's an integral leader of today!

Sam Chand
A friend of Nicholas John

CONTENTS

A LETTER FROM THE AUTHOR

The annuls of history will always be written because of the actions of our leaders. Leaders direct and dictate our history. Leaders have the singular effect of shaping our world—both past and present. That is how it has been, and this is how it will continue to be. So, if you want to change the world and make it a better place for all, you need to start with its leaders.

LEADERS HAVE THE SINGULAR EFFECT OF SHAPING OUR WORLD—BOTH PAST AND PRESENT. THAT IS HOW IT HAS BEEN, AND THIS IS HOW IT WILL CONTINUE TO BE. SO, IF YOU WANT TO CHANGE THE WORLD AND MAKE IT A BETTER PLACE FOR ALL, YOU NEED TO START WITH ITS LEADERS.

I believe that our world is a reflection of its leaders. I'm referring to all facets of our world—our families, homes, religious institutions, governments, schools, universities, hospitals, businesses and every other arena of our lives. They are all a reflection of their leaders.

We're all leaders in some shape or form. During our lifetime, we will inevitably take on some type of leadership role or at least have an opportunity to lead at something. It could be leading the school debate team, a sports team, the Scouts, a Sunday school class, a mega corporation or even your home and family. In all these instances, those you lead will be a reflection of you, its leader.

The teams or organizations you lead will have good and bad quality traits. Whether good or bad, all will ultimately be a reflection of you, its leader. I wish I could've personally met the great leadership architect, Dr. Myles Munroe, before he passed away. He had such foresight. In his book, *The Spirit of Leadership*, he provided the answer to a fundamental question: What is the number one need around the globe today? He answered,

There is nothing as elusive as leadership. *All the money in the world can make you rich, and all the power in the world can make you strong, but these things can never make you a leader.* You can inherit a fortune, but never leadership. Yet there is no greater need in our twenty-first century world than effective, competent leadership. Our greatest challenge is that of a leadership vacuum. The number one need all over the globe today is not money, social programs or even new governments. It is quality, moral, disciplined, principle-centered leadership. We need true leadership in our government, businesses, schools, civic institutions, youth communities, religious organizations, homes, and in every arena of our lives—including the disciplines of law, medicine, science, sports, and the media. Yet the search for *genuine leadership is becoming more difficult.*

The team or organization you're leading right now is a direct reflection of YOU—its leader. So, as you currently lead, what leadership traits are you reflecting?

What if you wanted to change the reflection of the world today? How would you go about doing it? The answer is simple—you would need to change what today's world leaders are reflecting. This is the challenge I've taken up in writing this book.

Leadership guru, Dr. John Maxwell, points out in *The Maxwell Leadership Bible* that principle-centered leaders who remain relevant do not merely react to their culture or changing surroundings. They base their leadership on tried-and-tested, timeless and universal principles. They remain relevant because they connect cultural changes to timeless truths. These timeless truths and principles act as a guide, a guard and a gauge. They guide us by keeping us on the right path, guard us by protecting our hearts and gauge us by evaluating who and where we are. I believe that these truths subconsciously direct leaders to focus on doing what is right. These are the genuine measures of a principle-centered leader's "unpublished" triple bottom line:

1) Responsibility before results

2) Character before conduct

3) Faithfulness before fruitfulness

Our world today measures its leaders primarily on results, conduct and fruitfulness. Therein lies our challenge. I've often experienced that these measurements, in isolation, will eventually result in the ruin of leaders and their organizations. This isn't necessarily the leader's fault because most leaders are taught to focus on *what* to do and not *who* they are. They are taught to *do*, not *be*. They are taught to focus on *results*, not *principles*. Dr. John Maxwell said, "Our leadership must flow out of our very being, a natural outgrowth of what we have incarnated. And yet most leaders struggle at exactly this point. By definition, most leaders are result-oriented." Therefore, maybe they are not so principle-oriented.

We all know the famous bedtime story of the three little pigs. The first little pig built his house with straw. The second little pig built his house with sticks. The third little pig built his house with bricks. Then along came the big, bad wolf. He got to the first little pig's house built with straw, and he huffed and he puffed and he blew the house down. Next, the big, bad wolf got to the second little pig's house built with sticks, and he huffed and he puffed and he blew the house down. Finally, the big, bad wolf got to the third little pig's house built with bricks. He huffed and he puffed three times, but guess what? The big, bad wolf could not blow the third little pig's house down.

If the three little pigs were leaders in our world today, which little pig would you want to lead you and keep the big, bad wolves away? Yes, you'd want the pig who had built his house of bricks.

PREPARING INTEGRAL LEADERS OF TOMORROW

I believe that people in the world today are looking for two things from their leaders: (1) a solid foundation and (2) the ability to lead with the right heart. In essence, people want quality, moral, disciplined and principle-centered leadership. Then, when the big, bad wolf comes a knocking, it will not be able to blow down the families, homes, religious institutions, governments, schools, universities, hospitals, businesses or any other arena that the little pig leads.

I BELIEVE THAT PEOPLE IN THE WORLD TODAY ARE LOOKING FOR TWO THINGS FROM THEIR LEADERS: (1) A SOLID FOUNDATION AND (2) THE ABILITY TO LEAD WITH THE RIGHT HEART.

Right now, as I add the finishing touches to this book, the world is in the midst of the COVID-19 crisis that has infected millions and led to hundreds of thousands of people dying. Our lives changed overnight as we began dealing with the biggest social and economic crisis that the human race has had to deal with in the past one hundred years. In such times, we all look to leaders to guide and assure us that everything is going to be okay. The crisis is testing the foundations and hearts of global leaders in every aspect of society: nations, governments, medical and healthcare institutions, educational institutions, religious institutions, business organizations, social welfare organizations, security and social services and every other organization that you can think of that keeps our daily lives going. We're all wondering, when the pages of the history books have been finally written, if the current crop of global leaders will have passed the ultimate test of saving the lives of millions of people across the world?

By writing this book, I knew I could do little to help the current generation of leaders, but I knew that I could get involved in preparing integral leaders of tomorrow. Firstly, I want to help future leaders build solid foundations by navigating them through the common leadership challenges they will encounter during their leadership journeys. Secondly, I want to focus on their heart development because integral leadership is all about the heart.

The title of this book, **PILOT**, is an acronym for **P**reparing **I**ntegral **L**eaders **O**f **T**omorrow. Hopefully the title is apt for the eventual meaning and purpose of my life. I may not be able to make a significant impact on today's leaders, but I'm certainly going to try to help shape the reflection of the world tomorrow by helping to shape the reflection of tomorrow's leaders.

This book focuses on addressing the leadership vacuum that exists in our world today. A vacuum of quality, moral, disciplined and principle-centered leadership. A vacuum of leaders with integrity. It may be too late to address the leadership vacuum that currently exists, but we can try to influence the leadership of tomorrow in some small way by Preparing Integral Leaders Of Tomorrow, today.

WHAT WILL YOU GET OUT OF THIS BOOK?

A wise friend once told me that "Before you can have a great steak, you need to have a great cow," and "A skyscraper begins with a great foundation." This book, **PILOT**, is the foundation for skyscrapers. In it you will find timeless and priceless building blocks to help you build a solid foundation of future leadership as you embark, or continue, on your leadership journey. **PILOT** will keep the big, bad wolf from blowing your house down. **PILOT** is a prerequisite for great leaders. If you have a desire to live a meaningful and purposeful life and leave a lasting memory on earth as a true leader, then this book will certainly help you achieve this.

Everyone talks about life purpose. Honestly, my life's purpose continues to be uncovered on the journey of self-discovery. But, while on this journey, I'm sure that it's headed in the direction of helping young leaders. It has taken me years of detours to get to this point. While I wish I had gotten here sooner, I'm glad I'm here now, and I'm quietly confident that *Preparing Integral Leaders of Tomorrow* may just be my meaning and purpose in this life.

PILOT represents my first real step towards embracing my meaning and purpose. Therefore, this book holds special significance. I pray it will be the catalyst to many future leaders who wish to prepare well for their leadership journeys.

So, thank you for picking up this book. I trust you will enjoy this **PILOT** journey together with me.

God bless,
Nicholas John

CHAPTER 1

THE JOURNEY TOWARDS PILOT

*When I'm in the sky, I feel God so close, and I
know that I can do the impossible!*

love to fly. I feel so safe and at peace when I'm in an airplane high above the earth. Spending the last twenty years of my life flying across the globe has been a privilege. I average six to eight flights a month. Once I did ten flights in a week! However, before you assume my life is glamorous, I suggest you watch the movie *Up in the Air* with George Clooney. This will give you a better understanding of the so-called glamorous lives that jet-setters lead. One day, I'm going to write a book called *The Travel Guide for Dummies* based on my many travel experiences, frustrations and learnings.

Throughout the years, I've come to realize that one of the coolest jobs in the world must be that of a commercial airline pilot. Think about it. You get paid to travel the world, you wear smart uniforms, people call you Captain, you get the best seats in the house, you don't have to wait in lines and people trust and respect you. Is it starting to sound appealing to you as well?

However, let's take a closer look at what is required to become a pilot:

- The first thing you need is a bachelor's degree in a field related to aeronautics.
- Regardless of a major, pilots must also complete coursework in physics, aeronautical engineering, mathematics and English.
- To get certified as a commercial pilot, you'll need to log close to two thousand hours in the air. That is a lot of flying! Let's put this into perspective—if a pilot flew eight hours every day for five days a week, he/she may still not achieve this target in one year, so there is no way a pilot can do all that flying quickly.
- They must pass a written knowledge exam which includes sections specifically related to the instruments on an airplane's dashboard.
- They must pass a physical exam, which includes having vision correctible to 20/20, good hearing and no physical issues that would stop them from doing their jobs.
- Individual airlines have their own requirements regarding drug testing, mental stability, physical fitness.
- Once hired, pilots spend another couple of months being trained in the procedures of their specific airlines. Even then, most new hires are brought on as co-pilots.

All in all, it could take you between four and seven years just to become an entry-level pilot.

While every commercial aircraft crew member has an important function, there is none greater than that of the pilot. The pilot is responsible for everything that occurs on the ground and during the flight, right up until the plane is safely parked again. According to the article "What Airline Pilots Do," posted on the website www.jobmonkey.com, pilots' responsibilities focus on safety: "Pilots are responsible for the operation of the aircraft, the safety of the passengers and crew members, and all flight decisions once in the air. Their primary concern, however, is the safety of the plane and passengers." That isn't all, though. JobMonkey goes on to list the following: "They must maintain a highly professional image in both conduct and personal appearance, and communicate with the passengers and crew during flights."

- "They must be trustworthy and have a high degree of integrity."
- "They check the weather, then plot a flight plan."
- "During flight, they constantly watch instruments, make adjustments," report to air traffic control stations on route and talk to the tower at the destination.
- Pilots typically report to work several hours "before departure in order to meet with flight crew and review weather and airport conditions."
- "The captain then goes through a series of safety checklists of switches and instruments in the cockpit with the first officer" (or co-pilot).
- "Every instrument is checked and double-checked."

- "In addition, the captain communicates with the air traffic controller and the ground crew in preparation for" take-off.
- During take-off and landing and while in flight, pilots continue communicating with one another, as well as with the air traffic controllers.
- The hardest parts of the flight are take-off and landing.
- Pilots are often required to stay away from home for extended periods.
- Their schedules often change and may be highly irregular.
- Mental stress is often high for pilots, somewhat worsened by jet lag for those who fly internationally.

Consider the consequences of a pilot failing in any of these duties? *There is a significantly high risk that people could die!* That's a lot of responsibility. Often, we don't even get to see or thank these pilots. Yet, for years these pilots have been flying us around the world to safely get to our destinations. Therefore, if I were to summarize the makings of a good pilot, I would say the following:

- A good pilot is well *prepared* and expertly *trained* to navigate the many challenges that could be faced along the journey.
- A good pilot has a *heart* for people—caring and protecting the safety of others at all times.

This got me thinking. . . . *What if leaders could be developed in* **PILOT** *school and go through a similar preparation and development process as that of pilots? What if we could replicate the process by preparing and training leaders of tomorrow?* How? First, leaders would be provided with the expert building blocks required to navigate their leadership journey. Secondly, the future leaders' hearts would be shaped to protect and care for people at all times.

Thus began my quest to find the most important qualities required to become truly inspirational leaders.

MY LEADERSHIP JOURNEY

Throughout my life, I've had many experiences working with great, and not so great, leaders. These experiences have acted as subtle building blocks, unconsciously shaping me into who I am today. I developed a passion for closely studying great leaders and searching for clues as to what makes them great. With each relationship and learning experience, I found joy in sharing what I was learning with others, and I grew passionate about empowering future leaders.

I wish I'd learned these leadership clues and lessons earlier in my life as I would've been better prepared to handle many of the failures I've experienced on my leadership journey. It would've saved me a lot of time, money and pain. But I'm also deeply grateful for these experiences and for the leaders who have impacted and shaped my life, some more positively than others. Nevertheless, all my experiences have played a vital part in my discovery of the most important qualities that every great and successful leader needs to possess.

One of my life-shaping experiences involved my childhood hero— Wessel Johannes "Hansie" Cronje. For those non-cricket enthusiasts, Hansie was the legendary captain of the South African cricket team in the 1990s. I idolized him. He was a fearless, natural born leader on the cricket pitch. Under his leadership, the team took on the many great sides of the world with significant success. His leadership style and character spilled over onto the team—he prided himself on being the fittest cricketer in the world and one that had a never-say-die attitude. Hansie was also the first South African cricketer to put real fear in the great Australian leg spinner, Shane Warne. Who could ever forget the famous innings at Wanderers Stadium in Johannesburg in 1994 where he carted Warne all around the field with his blistering batting? In 2016, Warne, who had ended his career as one of the greatest leg spinners of all time, mentioned Cronje as one of the best batsmen he had ever bowled to.

I'll never forget the first time I met Hansie while I was a student at the University of Natal in Durban, South Africa. The university held a Christian seminar, and the guest speaker line-up featured Andrew Hudson and Jonty Rhodes (two internationally famous Durban-born South African cricket stars) and Hansie. After the seminar, I fortuitously used a secret passage that students sneakily used to get to the pool room. To my amazement, there was Hansie. He was all alone, quietly leaning against a wall. I was starstruck! The Durban crowds were obviously so obsessed with getting closer glimpses of their local heroes that they had forgotten about Hansie. I nervously walked up to him, and he greeted me with a smile and handshake. I can't remember what he said to me, as there was such an aura about him, but I knew that I was in the presence of a truly great and inspirational leader.

The 1990s was a great period for South African cricket and, as a young fan, I couldn't get enough of it. I even pretended to be sick on a few Sundays in order to skip church and stay at home to watch an international match. Growing up as a PK (pastor's kid), missing Sunday church was the biggest sin. However, later in life, I realized that it wasn't cricket I was obsessed with. It was Hansie as our leader. Cricket for me centered on Hansie. There was a famous t-shirt that all cricket fans wore that had the following words on the front: "Cricket is not just a matter of life and death; it's more important than that." Cricket and life in those days were great, and it all was because of Hansie. Then, one of the greatest tragedies in the history of South African sport unfolded.

Many South Africans sorrowfully remember the day in 2000 when Hansie admitted to match-fixing and taking bribes from Indian bookmakers. It was the day cricket died for many in South Africa—including me. It wasn't the match-fixing that tore me apart. It was Hansie's conduct that made me, an innocent follower of a great leader, lose all hope and passion in the sport I had loved.

I vividly remember being so angry when the King Commission blatantly accused Hansie of match-fixing.

Hansie responded on April 9, 2000: "I want to make it one hundred percent clear that I deny ever receiving any sum of money during the one-day international series in India. I want to also make it absolutely clear I have never spoken to any member of the team about throwing a game."

"Hansie said that he didn't do it, so why don't they just leave him alone?" I barked at the radio while driving to work. Hansie would never have done such a thing, and I was standing one hundred percent behind him—our leader—against these vultures trying to accuse him of wrongdoing. But two days later, Hansie confessed that he'd been dishonest and that he had indeed taken money to share information with Indian bookmakers.

I chose to share this story in such detail because this was one of many experiences in my life where a leader whom I had allowed my heart to love, follow and respect failed me.

When I heard of Hansie's death in 2002, I didn't shed a tear because of the wounds that were still healing. Hansie stole my love for the game of cricket—a game that I still don't follow with much interest.

Hansie was only the beginning of many leaders I'd encounter in my life who would teach me some not-so-positive qualities. I started to learn about the obstacles in life that could cause even the greatest leaders to fall from grace on their leadership journeys.

I can also vividly recall when I was wrongfully accused by some church leaders of lying, cheating and stealing. While the accusations hurt, it was once again the conduct of the leaders that shocked and hurt me the most. Their words and behavior caused me to think, *Are they really leaders? Is this what being a leader is all about? Is this what leadership looks like?* I was confused and disillusioned.

Growing up in South Africa, I got accustomed to seeing leaders constantly in the spotlight for unscrupulous behavior. I'm not into politics, but when leaders of African countries that have extremely high unemployment rates continue to accumulate personal riches, live lives of luxury and conduct themselves in a manner detrimental to their followers, any reasonable person would begin to question their morality. It doesn't make sense! Actually, it makes one feel sick.

However, I still have hope because while these painful experiences continued, there were also many leaders who taught me many wonderful lessons in leading—lessons that have helped shape me into the leader I am today.

THE EARLY DAYS

Growing up in a small Indian community toward the end of apartheid in South Africa during the 1980s and 1990s, there were three significant people in my life that I will forever be indebted to for making me believe that leaders can have a positive influence in people's lives. They shaped my dream of developing leaders who are, in fact, just like them. These three people were my grandfather, my father and my mother. I've closely studied some of the leadership qualities that I believe made them great.

The first, my grandfather, was someone whom I fondly looked up to. He was an ordinary barber, but I learned so much from visiting him regularly at his barbershop in the city of Durban. My grandfather was a no-nonsense type of person. He was also a preacher, so you did not dare disturb his preaching on a Sunday morning. He was tough, disciplined and structured—from getting up very early every morning to pray, to the precise way his scissors had to be set after each customer's visit to his barbershop, to the meticulous way he prepared his sermons. But inside his tough exterior was a BIG heart for God and his family. I always found a way to get into his heart. My grandfather made sure that my dad clearly understood that he needed to finance a university education for me. He was adamant that I needed a good education. Nobody in my dad's family, which included nine siblings and plenty of grandchildren, had ever gone to university. I would be the first.

My grandfather had great foresight and, as mentioned, was exceptionally disciplined—two qualities for leading that I would come to learn and adopt in my life. He didn't have much in the sense of material wealth, but he gave me those two stand-out leadership qualities of foresight and discipline. What I'm doing today is largely due to his influence.

The second, my dad, is similar to my grandfather. He also has a hard exterior but is an even bigger softy at heart than my grandfather. He comes across as this stubborn tough guy who is set in his ways, but he just loves people and wants to make sure that every person he meets gets to heaven. My grandfather was a pastor, and my father is still a pastor in the local church we attend. I've learned two valuable lessons from both of them for leading in life:

1) "For with God nothing will be impossible" (Luke 1:37, NKJV) and

2) Leadership is a heart issue. Genuine leadership comes from the heart. If you want to develop as a leader, then you need to first develop or change your heart.

NEVER GIVE UP

There are many other characteristics of leadership that I learned from my dad. Another key was to "Never give up" because God is always with you. My dad has been through tough things in his life from being attacked, stabbed and left for dead when I was just a little boy, to being unfairly retrenched from his corporate job, to surviving two heart attacks, to overcoming cancer. Yet, he has still never given up. He still wants to make a difference in people's lives.

My dad lost his job as I was heading into my final year of university. Our family income dried up, but Dad (and Mum) did everything to ensure I finished my degree. It was a humbling season for all of us. My dad started a business selling toilet paper to retail stores to support the family during this time. I still have nightmares about the many weekends that Kirbashnee, my then girlfriend now wife, and I sat in my dad's bakkie selling toilet paper to supplement our income. I was so embarrassed and always sent Kirbashnee to serve those wanting to buy toilet paper. My friend Mike Robertson, a pastor from Visalia, California, always tells me that my beautiful wife must have married for money. He is wrong. I sold toilet paper!

BE HUMBLE

My dad also taught me to be humble. This has probably been my biggest lesson in leading. I struggled with humility in my earlier years. I'll never forget the time I had a meeting with a senior pastor of a church who was a little too overbearing for me. After the meeting, I drove home to find my dad in his shorts, lying on the grass pampering our dogs. That day, my dad reminded me that life isn't about fame; it's about being humble and doing the right things for God.

My dad wanted to give me two things in life: God and an education. He certainly has. But he has also instilled in me so much more, including many important qualities required to become a great leader.

JUST GET ON WITH IT

Finally, there is my mum who has also shown me so many great leadership lessons in life. The one thing that stands out is that she taught me to "Just get on with it." Keep moving forward! When Dad lost his job, Mum just got on with it. When Dad had his heart attacks, Mum just got on with it. When Dad got cancer, Mum just got on with it. She has a steely interior, and nothing distracts her from taking care of all of us. I definitely get my "drama queen" habits from my dad, not from my mum. She's never embarrassed to do whatever it takes for us—from loading and offloading toilet paper, to selling hot dogs to factory workers during lunch breaks, to bargaining for the best deal while shopping. She is always authentic—a key trait of any great leader.

These three human beings formed a solid foundation of learning for me. They taught me many great leadership traits and encouraged me to believe that leaders can make a genuine and positive difference in people's lives. My passion to teach these leadership lessons and help develop future leaders was birthed during my early years. But I still did not fully understand or realize it until I stepped into the next chapter of my life.

ENTERING THE REAL WORLD

I had a good foundation for life from my youth. While the joy of finding new beacons of true leadership continued, I was about to gain more insight into leading as I began my corporate career in 1998 with Deloitte & Touche—a global leader in professional services. It was during this season that I began earnestly searching the world for more qualities that defined great leaders.

It was also during this time that I became disillusioned. Perhaps what I was looking for didn't exist? I was trying to find the Superman of leadership—someone who possessed the DNA for all the perfect qualities of great leadership, but all I saw around me were leaders who were failing. I only encountered fraud, corruption, scandal, lawlessness, immorality and selfish gain in leaders of governments, corporate organizations, religious institutions, society and the world at large. It was enough to make me sick, and I started asking some sobering questions:

- Why are our current leaders letting us down?
- From where will the next generation of leaders come?
- When will these leaders arise?
- What type of leaders will they be?
- Who is equipping these leaders to lead right?
- What will our leaders of tomorrow look like?

As a young man, I desperately wanted to make a positive difference. Maybe my naïve upbringing led me to believe it, but I believed that by serving leaders I could make that difference in the world. I knew if I wanted to make an impact, then I'd have to impact the world's leaders. But how? I knew it was nearly impossible to have any influence on the current leaders around me. Who was I that they would want to listen to the valuable lessons in leadership that I was learning?

Then it finally dawned on me. I could make an impact. What if I could help shape *tomorrow's* leaders—starting now? Imagine if I could help up-and-coming leaders realize their leadership potential and help them grow their leadership capabilities? There is still time; there is still hope.

I could help develop our future leaders by making sure they understood the vital elements for leading. I could help them comprehend:

- What it really means to lead people.
- What should be inside a leader's heart.

- Why integrity is important for a leader.
- Why character matters most.
- What it means to be whole.
- What it means to have influence over people.
- Why leaders need to be brave.
- Why leaders need to care.
- Why leadership is actually serving.

My journey was starting to make sense and take shape. I was learning why I had this passion for leadership and what I wanted to do with it. But there was still an important puzzle piece holding me back—I was still too young and inexperienced. I was just starting my leadership journey, and I still had so much to learn. Why would people even want to listen to me? I had no credibility in the discipline of leadership.

THE VISION MADE CLEAR

It was during this time, around 2009, when I met Samuel R. Chand—otherwise known as Dr. Sam Chand to so many people across the world. I believe that God allowed him to come into my life at the perfect time.

He has single-handedly taken what has been in my heart since I was a young, impressionable man and provided the focus, direction, plan and anchor to help me start fulfilling my vision of developing quality leaders all over the world. And he continues to do so today. Sam's life mission is "helping others succeed," and he is certainly helping me succeed in my life's journey!

A few years back, he encouraged me to start a company called LeaderGrow. LeaderGrow is a leadership company with a vision to help young adults realize their leadership potential and grow their leadership capability. The aim is for people to take what is in their hearts and equip themselves for self-leadership and the leadership of others. LeaderGrow is focused on the creation and facilitation of quality, integrous and purpose-driven leaders, so that collectively we can contribute to the development of a strong culture of leadership. We help people become leaders. We provide individuals with the training, encouragement and coaching to become truly inspirational leaders of tomorrow. Our leadership experience removes the divide. Our leadership ethos deals with relationships at their core; transactions are secondary.

Dr. Chand is my partner, mentor and friend, and he has been hugely instrumental in my writing this book. He taught me first-hand some of the leadership lessons you'll read about; therefore, credit must be given to him for his contributions, and for his and his wife, Brenda's, input in my and my family's lives.

PILOT IS BORN

When LeaderGrow was established, one of the first initiatives I started was a learning program to prepare young leaders for the challenges that they would face along their leadership journeys. My aim was to help steer them through some of the inevitable obstacles and roadblocks. The learning program is based on leadership principles, building blocks or personal traits that we believe every leader needs to master. Dr. Chand has also written extensively on some of these leadership principles in his book *What's Shaking Your Ladder?*

With his expert knowledge and my own personal leadership lessons gleaned from over twenty years leading in the corporate world, the program provides real-life experiences to help future leaders. It's a concrete program that ensures students get more than just a set of theories. It's principles are based on personal leadership experiences and what we've learned from the work we've done with many world-class leaders from all walks of life, over many years and from all around the world. The principles aren't centered on competency but rather on behavioral aspects, so the focus is on developing each leader as a person.

This learning program was given the name **PILOT**—an acronym for **P**reparing **I**ntegral **L**eaders **O**f **T**omorrow. **PILOT** was born to be a foundational leadership program designed to equip and empower future leaders with the building blocks that will remain relevant throughout their leadership journey. Irrespective of where leaders are on their journey, **PILOT** provides a solid foundation to make their journeys successful.

Whether you're a young leader finding your path, a seasoned CEO or senior pastor, these principles will outlive you, as well as generations of leaders to come. I've listed the full list of building blocks we cover in our **PILOT** program at the end of this book.

You'll notice that the title of this book is also **PILOT**, which is no coincidence. Its objective is to help Prepare Integral Leaders Of Tomorrow, so I'll cover some of the leadership learning blocks taught in our **PILOT** program. However, this book isn't intended to be a complete **PILOT** program, which is typically run over an eight-month period. But I can assure you that I've incorporated enough in this book to give you a good understanding of the building blocks you'll need to master along your leadership journey.

Now that this is all said and done, I'd like to welcome you aboard this **PILOT** flight. I hope to get you to your leadership destination safely. The captain has turned on the "fasten seat belt" sign, so take your seat. I advise you to keep your seat belts fastened throughout the flight, as we will likely enter areas of turbulence that may cause instability during the leadership journey. Make sure your seat is in an upright position to maintain the right attitude for the trip. Fold-away tray tables represent any obstacles that may impede you from developing throughout this flight. This is a non-smoking flight, as we need all of our future leaders on board to be fit and healthy. Cabin crew, prepare the cabin for take-off.

Enjoy your **PILOT** journey with me.

CHAPTER 2

PREPARING YOURSELF WELL TO LEAD WELL

By failing to prepare, you are preparing to fail.
—Benjamin Franklin

I f you fail to prepare, be prepared to fail. This is my version of the famous quote by Benjamin Franklin who was one of the Founding Fathers of the United States. In any journey in life, the preparation phase is often forgotten by the time you get to a journey's end. Also, many of us do not want to waste the time—or may not have the patience—to worry about preparing for our journey's end. Yet, preparing is the most vital part of any journey. So, too, with our **PILOT** journey. It is a journey that has already had many years of preparation. In fact, right now, I'm still preparing for the next chapter of the **PILOT** journey.

Remember that **PILOT** is an acronym for Preparing Integral Leaders Of Tomorrow, and as previously mentioned, I will use this acronym as the key framework throughout this book.

In this chapter as well as the next, we'll look at the first letter in the acronym **PILOT**—the **P** for **P**reparing.

PREPARING TO LEAD NATIONS

Nelson Rolihlahla Mandela, fondly known as Madiba to any South African, was an anti-apartheid revolutionist. According to "International Nelson Mandela Day 2020: History and Significance of the Day," an article posted at India.com, he was also a political leader and philanthropist who served as the president of South Africa from 1994 to 1999. Madiba was a hero to many in our nation, and he left an indelible mark on my life as a young man growing up in a post-apartheid South Africa. In 1962, Madiba was arrested for conspiring to overthrow the state and was sentenced to life imprisonment during the Rivonia Trial. Madiba served twenty-seven years in prison, initially on Robben Island, and later in Pollsmoor Prison and Victor Verster Prison.

Let me say that again—the great Nelson Rolihlahla Mandela spent twenty-seven years in prison!

Have you ever wondered what was happening during those twenty-seven years? Madiba was PREPARING to become the first democratic president and the first black president of the Republic of South Africa.

I visited Robben Island many years ago and had the privilege of visiting Madiba's famous prison cell. It was a small cell, about four square meters, with thin blankets that served as a bed on the floor and an iron bucket for a toilet. He was allowed one visitor a year for thirty minutes and worked in the lime quarry daily. Madiba spent eighteen years at Robben Island prison—a time described by the PBS documentary "The Long Walk of Nelson Mandela" as the "crucible which transformed him." He learned to speak Afrikaans, the language of the enemy, so that he could communicate with his oppressors. "When you speak to a man and he understands, he does so with his mind, but if you speak to him in his language he understands with his heart," Madiba said.

With his intelligence, charm and dignified defiance, he won over even the harshest prison officials during those eighteen years. He assumed leadership of his comrades and emerged from the process of preparation as a mature leader—one who would fight and win great political battles that would ultimately unite a nation. The story of Madiba demonstrates the importance of preparing for future leadership. Preparing to be a leader of tomorrow is a process that even the greatest leaders go through.

There are other eminent examples who have inspired me along my journey and helped me prepare as a leader. My mentor, Dr. Chand, grew up in a pastor's home in India but moved to the United States in 1973 to become a student at Beulah Heights University. At a certain point, his funding was withdrawn, and he had to work as a janitor, dishwasher and cook at the university just to earn some extra cash. He later returned to Beulah Heights University in 1989 but this time as its president. Under his leadership, Beulah Heights University became the country's largest predominantly African-American Bible

College. Dr. Chand is currently a leadership architect and change strategist serving pastors and business leaders around the world. He personally consults, mentors and coaches pastors from some of the largest churches. He also speaks regularly at leadership conferences, churches, corporations, leadership roundtables, minister's conferences, seminars and other leadership development venues. He was named in the Top Global Leadership Gurus list. But many will never know about those seasons of preparing that he went through to get to where he is now.

In preparing for my journey, I also learned a lot from growing up in church and studying key biblical characters who were chosen as leaders to fulfill big assignments for God. Some famous examples include Noah who prepared for 120 years before building his ark for the floods, Abraham who waited for twenty-five years before he received the promise of his son Isaac and Joseph who spent thirteen years in prison before he became second-in-command in the land of Egypt. However, the biblical character who is closest to my heart, and who best demonstrates the necessity of preparing well to lead, is Moses.

God gave His servant Moses one of the toughest assignments of any leader. He was to lead nearly two million people from the bonds of an Egyptian pharaoh to God's chosen Promised Land. When God gave Moses the promise that he'd been chosen to lead the children of Israel into a land flowing with milk and honey, it was the beginning of a journey that would take forty years—and Moses was already eighty years old. It's not so much the assignment given to Moses that fascinates and captures my imagination; it's the process of preparing him for the assignment. In order to fulfill the assignment, Moses had to go through a harsh and long preparation process. His preparation process can be broken down into three segments of forty years each. Let's review each of them.

Moses Learns He Is Somebody (Years 0 to 40)

Moses spent the first forty years of his life being prepared, schooled and trained in the ways of the Egyptians in the courts of Pharaoh. You may be familiar with the Bible story of Moses where Pharoah's daughter found Moses (a Hebrew child) floating in a basket along the Nile River and adopted him. She named him Moses meaning "I drew him out of the water." Moses was therefore the adopted grandson of the king. He received the finest education and was part of Egyptian royalty.

Moses Learns He Is Nobody (Years 41 to 80)

It was during this period that Moses started realizing the burdens of his birth people. When he saw an Egyptian beating a Hebrew, he killed the Egyptian. Pharaoh sought to kill Moses for this deed, but he fled to Midian. Moses had tried to deliver his people using the ways of the Egyptians, but it was not God's way. So God banished him to the land of Midian for additional preparation. The Midianites (people of the land of Midian) were from the seed of Abraham, and Abraham is also regarded as the father of the nation of Israel.

Moses spent these forty years tending sheep in the wilderness before his profound experience of God appearing to him in a "burning bush." Moses was in a period of forced obscurity. Yes, he got married and was part of a family, but God used this time to shape and prepare him for his ultimate assignment. The definition of obscurity is the quality or condition of being unknown. It refers to life outside the limelight, serving in the background without recognition and having something to offer on a smaller stage.

During these forty years, God prepared Moses by teaching him the trade of shepherding sheep. He learned how to move sheep around the barren land to places where water and grass could be found.

Moses Learns that God Can Use a Nobody (Years 81 to 120)

During this segment, Moses learned that God can do great things with a nobody. Moses spent the next forty years of his life finally fulfilling his assignment by leading the people to the foot of the Promised Land. The desert was a place of preparation for one of the greatest assignments ever given to one man. Moses was getting prepared during the second segment of his life to spend another forty years in the same environment to lead a stubborn and willful people out of slavery.

In all of the above accounts, from Madiba to Moses, the most critical time in their lives were those periods of *forced obscurity*—in prison, as a janitor and in the desert—where they were alone, broken, discouraged and, at times, even disillusioned and defeated. These periods of forced obscurity were simply preparing these great men to fulfill the big assignments in their lives. The concept of preparing is true for every assignment in our own lives. Whether we want to shed a few extra pounds, climb Mount Everest or simply learn to drive, the process of preparing is the secret to success for every leader.

PREPARING YOURSELF AS A LEADER

In our **PILOT** program, we treat this process of preparing as vitally important to developing integral leaders of tomorrow. If I were to unpack the entire module on preparing, it would be a book on its own. In these two chapters I'll attempt to share some of the more necessary core principles of preparing that may be of benefit to you. I believe these core principles are critical for every leader as they highlight the importance of preparing well in order to fulfill the big assignments in your life.

I'd like to reiterate that these core principles are necessary and vital in reaching your end goal. Preparing will always be a continuous process; therefore, I want to focus on a leader's entire journey (from beginning to end) to ensure that you get to *your* end and—most importantly—that you finish well.

Let's consider these five principles required during the stages of preparing.

1) Leaders prepare themselves first.

This is often a difficult task in the twenty-first century because we need instant gratification. Everything has to be big, and everything has to be fast. For example, all major corporations tend to review and report their results on a monthly basis, so their leaders are constantly under scrutiny and in the spotlight. This makes the process of preparing even more difficult for today's leaders as results need to be immediate.

However, the life of a farmer is a good example of the importance of preparing to realize an outcome. A farmer cannot harvest until he first prepares the soil and the ground to sow the seed. In fact, there are eight major steps of preparing for a harvest that a farmer typically goes through—(1) crop selection, (2) land preparation, (3) seed selection, (4) seed sowing, (5) irrigation, (6) crop growth, (7) fertilizing and, finally, (8) harvesting. Harvesting is the *event*, while the first seven steps are the *process* of preparing for the event.

HARVESTING IS THE EVENT, WHILE THE FIRST SEVEN STEPS ARE THE PROCESS OF PREPARING FOR THE EVENT.

This analogy is also true for developing integral leaders of tomorrow. Often potential leaders will attend many "events" during their lifetimes to learn more about leadership. I know I have. While this is commendable and even recommended, the stark reality is that leadership development is not an *event*. It's an ongoing *process* of preparing for harvesting. The best results always come to those who are most prepared.

THE BEST RESULTS ALWAYS COME TO THOSE WHO ARE MOST PREPARED.

We saw earlier how three effective leaders started preparing before they recognized it as such. And, that preparation did not happen in a day or even over a few days, but rather over many years—not through an event or events, but through a continual and ongoing process.

Great leaders are prepared in a slow cooker, not in a microwave oven. The long-awaited goal is less important than the work happening inside the leader while he or she waits. Waiting matures us, levels our perspective and broadens our understanding. Tests of time determine whether we can endure seasons of preparation that are seemingly unfruitful. I can testify to this as I endured these seasons when nothing seemed to be happening. They indicate whether we can recognize and seize opportunities that come our way. They also provide accurate assessments of whether we will last the journey and make it to the end.

2) Preparing is not planning.

I was taught early in my leadership journey that there is a vast difference between preparing and planning. You plan for a wedding day, but you prepare for a lifetime of marriage. You plan for a baby, but you prepare for a family. Preparing is not planning.

Planning is concrete and focused, and it's usually for an event. For example, planning for a job interview or planning for a wedding. It's usually for a single occasion. Planning lets you know what you will be doing on a particular day or over set period of time.

Preparation, on the other hand, is abstract, ambiguous and broad. For example, all the years in school and university studying towards your qualifications have gotten you to the job interview. Preparation allows for forethought on how to deal with success as well as failure. Preparation isn't only *what* you know but also *whom* you build relationships with. I'll refer to these concepts in more detail later in this chapter.

There's a famous quote that says, "Planning leads to awareness. Preparation leads to readiness," and it makes perfect sense why Abraham Lincoln is business coach Jon Dwoskin's role model. Dwoskin quotes Lincoln on his website *The JonDwoskin Experience* as having said, "I will prepare, and someday my chance will come," and "Give me six hours to chop down a tree, and I will spend the first four sharpening the axe." Planning is good, but preparation is even better. Preparation gets you ready to actually do the work.

3) Preparing starts with finding your focus.

"Finding Focus" is one of the key modules in our **PILOT** program aimed at helping leaders of tomorrow understand WHO they are. Finding your focus comes from knowing and understanding your WHO (who you are), which is the first step in preparing to be a future leader.

As a future leader you need to first find focus or, in other words, find and maintain what is important to you. This is the biggest challenge faced at every level of leadership. Broken focus will be a key struggle throughout your leadership journey. By clearly understanding your main focus and WHAT is most important to you, boundaries can be put in place to avoid distractions. Finding and keeping your focus will be an ongoing challenge as you grow in leadership because growth multiplies distractions. Distractions will multiply in these five areas: people, places, programs, procedures and plans (the five Ps). These distractions slowly take over until the main thing often becomes the most neglected thing. You know what to do, but maintaining focus is difficult.

Let's try to understand focus a bit better. Focus comes from our WHO. What we focus on should always flow from our WHO. Once we define our WHO, WHAT we do will always flow from who we are. Simply put, the WHAT flows from the WHO.

Let's review this again:

- Focus comes from our WHO—who we are.
- Once we define our WHO, WHAT we do will always flow from WHO we are.
- The WHAT flows from the WHO.

This is true for leaders and also for the organizations they lead. The organization is a reflection of the leader's vision or *who* the leader is. How an organization accomplishes its vision is the *what* it does. However, an organization cannot do the *what* until it understands the *who*.

Simon Sinek, bestselling author of *Start With Why*, highlights the need to understand your *why*, as he puts it, in the same way I talk about your *who*. He uses a model that he calls The Golden Circle to explain how legendary leaders were able to achieve what others, who were just as smart and talented, were not.

In The Golden Circle (Figure 1), Sinek illustrates that every person's career operates on three levels. What we do, how we do it and why we do it. We all know what we do—the products or ideas we sell. Some of us know how we do it—the things that set us apart from our peers or competitors. But very few people can clearly articulate why we do what we do. *Why* is a purpose and goes deeper into understanding exactly what motivates and inspires us. Sinek says the *why* is grounded in the biology of human decision-making. The Golden Circle perfectly maps the way our brains work.

The outer section of The Golden Circle (the WHAT) corresponds to the outer circle of the brain (the neocortex). This is the part of

The Golden Circle

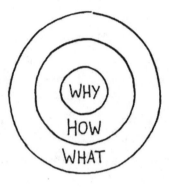

WHAT

Every organization on the planet knows WHAT they do. These are products they sell or the services they offer.

HOW

Some organizations know HOW they do it. These are the things that make them special or set them apart from their competition.

WHY

Very few organizations know WHY they do what they do. WHY is not about making money. That's a result. WHY is a purpose, cause or belief. It's the very reason your organization exists.

© 2017 Simon Sinek
from *Start With Why* by Simon Sinek

Figure 1: The Golden Circle—Simon Sinek (Start With Why)

the brain responsible for rational and analytical thought. It helps us understand facts and figures and is also responsible for language.

The middle sections of The Golden Circle (the WHY and HOW) correspond to the middle section of the brain (the limbic system). This is the part of the brain responsible for all our behavior and decision-making. It's also responsible for all feelings, like trust and loyalty. This is where our gut feelings come from. Sinek explains that this separation of abilities is the biological reason we sometimes find it difficult to put our feelings into words.

Once you understand your WHY, you'll be able to clearly articulate what makes you feel fulfilled. You will also understand what drives your behavior when you are at your natural best.

Perhaps by now you are asking, "What if I don't know my WHO or my WHY?" This brings me to the next important point.

Finding your WHO or your WHY is the first step in every influential leader's preparation process. It'll require you to search deep within yourself. It could take days, weeks, months or even many years (like me) to understand your WHO. Many people think they know who they are, but they often just know what they do and think that means they know who they are.

Here are some key questions that you should ask yourself to help you find your *WHO*:

- Who am I? (NOT What do I do?)
- If I were to die today, what would I most regret leaving unfinished?
- What is my meaning and purpose in life? Why do I exist?
- What do I spend hours thinking about?
- Why did I get out of bed this morning? What is driving me?
- What angers me the most? This could also be a clue to finding your *WHO*.

Finding your *WHO* is the most liberating feeling you will ever experience. It gives you clarity, as well as a sense of meaning and purpose in your life and in your calling as a leader. It's like a person with an eye condition who can only see the world as blurry images.

When they put on their prescription glasses, suddenly everything comes into focus. "I can see clearly now!" From this point on, *WHAT* you do in your life as a leader should always come from *WHO* you are.

Finding my *WHO* began in September 2009. I fondly and vividly remember this surreal vision of raising kings and priests. It was one of the few times in my life when it felt like God was prompting me into something. I'd had an interest in studying leaders and leadership principles from a young age. I always tried to emulate the many characteristics that I observed in my leaders. I also love helping and teaching people. My wife will tell you that I love to talk, and when I get an opportunity to teach, I can't stop talking!

Over the years, as I started unpacking this vision of raising kings and priests, I discovered that kings and priests were examples of two leadership types in the Old Testament in the Bible. Perhaps I was being called to help leaders. It was a slow metamorphosis of my *WHO*, but it started to feel right. It felt good doing it—I got that warm, fuzzy feeling you get in your tummy when you know something is right. It was liberating to have some clarity on my *WHO* and *WHY* in life. Little did I know, this was just the start of my extensive and intense preparation process.

Finding your *WHO* as a leader is about finding your *authenticity*. It's discovering your original intent and genuineness as a person. There are no more reasons to pretend to be who you are not. Why pretend to be like someone else for the sake of fitting in? My mentor asks, "You were born an original; why do you want to die a copy?"

Finding your *WHO* means finding your *YOU*, and there is only one unique *YOU*. The world is waiting in anticipation for you to find your *WHO* and for *YOU* to take your unique place in history.

THE WORLD IS WAITING IN ANTICIPATION FOR YOU TO FIND YOUR WHO AND FOR YOU TO TAKE YOUR UNIQUE PLACE IN HISTORY.

---

4) Preparing to Cast Your Vision.

You're on the journey of *finding* your WHO. Now you need to start preparing to cast the big vision for your life to *achieve* your WHO. I wish I'd learned more about preparing to cast my vision earlier in life. It would've saved me a lot of time and heartache, and lots of money.

LeaderGrow was initially called Dream Releaser Africa, and our signature **PILOT** program was referred to as the PLOT (Preparing Leaders of Tomorrow) program. You'll notice two things about our initial vision: (1) we were restricting our vision to Africa and (2) the key word "Integral" was missing in developing future leaders. We eventually got to where we wanted to be with our vision (almost three years later). I don't want you to make the same mistakes that I did. Let me take you through some vital principles in casting your vision. I did mostly the opposite of all of these principles when I initially started casting my vision and it cost me dearly.

First, when casting your vision, the power is not in the number of times you cast; it's in the perfect cast. Dr. Chand uses the analogy of fly fishing when explaining casting vision to future leaders. Below is an extract from his book *What's Shaking Your Ladder?*

Fly-fishing is different from the drop-your-pole-in-the-lake kind of fishing that many are familiar with. In fly-fishing, the key is in the casting. The best rod and reel and the perfect bait won't help. Unless the fisherman knows how to cast, he's not going to catch anything. The perfect cast involves both hands working at the same time, pulling and throwing simultaneously. I think. There is an important lesson from this analogy. The power isn't in the number of times you cast; the power is in the perfect cast. This is also true of vision casting. We can have the perfect vision, but unless we know how to cast that vision, it will never grab hold of anyone.

Vision casting is not announcing; it's more like recruiting. It's like recruiting investors to buy some shares in your company. If you are a business leader looking for investors, you need to sell the future benefits for the investor. When we cast our visions, we must think of it in the same way. We're not trying to inform people; we're trying to get people to invest. Vision casting is recruiting the right people to buy into you. When I first cast the vision for Dream Releaser Africa, I started by doing lots of announcements in large group settings. It failed miserably. However, with LeaderGrow, I began recruiting people in small settings on a one-on-one basis before I did any announcements in large settings.

Secondly, there are five types of people to whom you will be casting your vision. They can be broken down as follows:

Excited Embracers—two percent of the population

These people are excited to embrace your vision. They know you, they hear you, they get you and they support you. You don't need to give them all the details. They're filled with energy, they're excited and they're on top of things. Unfortunately, there are only a few of them. Excited Embracers make up approximately two percent of the population.

Early Embracers

Like the Excited Embracers, Early Embracers will embrace your vision early, though maybe not with as much zeal as the Excited Embracers. These people will stick with you as you work to make the vision a reality. Early Embracers make up approximately eighteen percent of the population.

Middlers

Middlers make up the largest group that you will cast your vision to. They make up approximately sixty percent of the population. These people hear your vision but need more time to think about it. They will not really make up their minds unless someone close to them convinces them. They may not be *against* your vision, but they are not sure and need convincing.

Late Embracers

Late Embracers have already decided that they do not support your vision. There may be a slim chance that later on, as your vision moves along, they change their minds, but it's still a long shot. They make up approximately eighteen percent of the population.

Never Embracers

Never Embracers are not fans of you or maybe even fans of most people. No matter what you try to do, they will never change their minds. They simply won't support you. Fortunately, they make up only two percent of the population.

As we prepare to cast our visions, we know now that the top twenty percent are strongly behind us, and the bottom twenty percent are against us. So, we need to target the Middlers, the sixty percent who haven't yet made up their minds. Unfortunately, what leaders generally do, myself included when I first launched Dream Releaser Africa, is to try to convince the below twenty percent to buy into their vision. We spend a massive amount of time, effort, money and other resources to try to win them over, while neglecting the top eighty percent.

There's a better way to do this:

- Ignore the below twenty percent—they're not going anywhere.
- Spend more time investing in the top twenty percent. They are for you and, by equipping them with more information and sharing your heart, they will become even greater ambassadors for your vision.
- Now use the top twenty percent to start engaging with the Middlers. You'll recall that Middlers are the people that need a little convincing, and the Early and Late Embracers can help you do this. Middlers will not be comfortable in large settings,

so they need to be recruited in informal settings—in the cafe-teria, at a coffee shop or over a casual lunch.

I read this in the Bible, which provides interesting insight into where we should devote our attention: "Do not give dogs what is sacred; do not throw your pearls to pigs. If you do, they may trample them under their feet, and turn and tear you to pieces" (Matthew 7:6, NIV). We're not referring to certain groups of people as pigs, but it's a good application of the above approach. "Pigs" will trample the soul of your vision. In other words, don't cast your vision to the bottom twenty percent because they're going to destroy your vision and turn on you. Leaders must learn to be strategic in vision casting. We have to prepare our messages for the people—the right type of people—people who support us and want to see our visions fulfilled.

5) Preparing to Surround Yourself with the Right Mentors.

I've been fortunate as I haven't had to deliberately search for men-tors. I'm thankful to God for His providence in this area of my life. In 2009, when I first had this thought to raise leaders, I didn't have a clue what to do, how to do it or where to start. It was during this season when God orchestrated my meeting Dr. Sam Chand, who would shape my future and purpose. I first met Dr. Chand through one of my spiritual mentors. Before then, I'd neither heard of nor seen him. In 2010, I used my growing credibility as a young partner at Deloitte to pitch the idea that maybe he could be the guest speaker at Deloitte's prestigious CEO roundtable events across South Africa. These were intimate events where the Deloitte CEO invited the CEOs of Deloitte's top clients to network with each other over a casual breakfast with a topical guest speaker. Deloitte happened to say yes to my idea, so Dr. Chand became the topical guest speaker who would be presenting to some of South Africa's top CEOs. While he was in South Africa, I was his chauffeur, transporting him back and forth to many of his speaking assignments in and around the city of Durban. I didn't realize that he would become a significant influence in my life as a mentor and coach.

There have been, and will be, many mentors in my life, and I mention some of them in this book. Sometimes, however, you'll also have mentors in your life that appear for a brief season. During that season, you may not pay attention to the impact they're subtly, yet enormously, making in your life. You may not notice either, but, later on, you'll realize what a significant role they've played in your life. In hindsight, I realize there were a few such people in my life. Perhaps even now, they haven't recognized their considerable impact. I now fondly recall three senior partners/directors at Deloitte—Danita de Swardt, Miles Crisp and Guy Brazier—who played this unassuming mentoring role in my life.

Danita was like a mother to me during my early days at Deloitte. She was also the person who promoted me (albeit not in title) to my first big role in leading a team in the 2000s. It was a period of transition in our Durban regional office where we did not have a senior partner overseeing our local division. Danita chose me to assist her in looking after the Durban regional office and team, which she took responsibility for in addition to her existing role of looking after the Johannesburg region where she lived. While I was never a partner in name or title, it was preparing me for the role of a director far in advance. Danita played that unassuming role of getting me on that track by preparing me in the background without being recognized or noticed.

Miles was a highly successful senior partner and also part of the executive team. Miles intuitively realized that I wasn't going to be a traditional partner, but that I had an entrepreneurial flair lurking inside me. Miles moved me into a little business within Deloitte called Tip-offs Anonymous. While Tip-offs Anonymous was owned by Deloitte, it was run separately as a small stand-alone business within the larger organization. Miles announced me as the chief operating officer reporting directly to then CEO, Guy Brazier. Guy and I were given the freedom to run Tip-offs Anonymous as entrepreneurs while having the safety net and protection of belonging to a large global conglomerate. We had our own company number, bank account and board of directors, and we could make our own decisions to grow this little company further. It was one of the best experiences and times of my life. This business grew to over 350 clients and became a global leader in its field. I eventually became CEO of Tip-offs Anonymous in 2010, which was my last position before I left Deloitte in 2012. Miles didn't know it at the time, but he was preparing me to one day run my own business—LeaderGrow.

Finally, there was a remarkable gentleman named Guy Brazier. Guy and his wife, Grace, probably had the biggest influence during my career at Deloitte. Guy was the CEO of Deloitte Tip-off Anonymous, as mentioned, and he was also the Regional Leader of the Deloitte Durban office during my time there. Guy taught me so many things, like how to prepare well financially for the future, and that relationships in business are vital. But his most important lesson was how to make people feel special, which was probably his greatest strength. I'll never forget how Guy and Grace welcomed both Kirbashnee and me into the Deloitte partnership back in 2007. They were so warm, and they made us feel so comfortable to be part of an elite group of partners and directors in a global firm. Guy was never shy to introduce me in any of his relationships. If there were someone who he thought would be beneficial for me to meet or who could help further my career, he would make that introduction happen. It was actually Guy who introduced me to Andrew Hudson, one of my cricket idols whom I referred to earlier.

A future leader's success is completely dependent on the type of mentors they surround themselves with. Mentors are people who, at various stages of your life, sharpen you and move you towards your destiny. The right mentors can be shortcuts to success in your life. You've seen that I've had many of these mentors at various stages of my own journey. So, let's take a look at some advantages of having mentors in your life.

Provision, Promotion and Protection

First, mentors are able to release three things in your life:

1) **Provision**—A mentor will supply certain key needs (tangible and intangible), e.g. knowledge, resources or relationships.

2) **Promotion**—A mentor will promote and lift you up by lending you his or her credibility, reputation and influence.

3) **Protection**—A mentor will protect you from pitfalls along your journey because that person has already been on the journey.

Butlers and Bakers

Secondly, your mentors act as *butlers* and *bakers* in unlocking the doors to your dreams.

A big part of realizing your dreams is to identify the *butlers* and the *bakers* that come into your life. Jentezen Franklin, the senior pastor of Free Chapel in Georgia, taught on the importance of butler and baker mentors in his life-changing book *Believe That You Can*.

The best example of *butler* and *baker* mentors can be found in the story of Joseph in the Bible. You can read the full account of Joseph in the book of Genesis from chapter thirty-seven to chapter fifty.

In this account, you will notice that Joseph was a big dreamer, and he dreamt of greatness in his life. Joseph had a dream that one day he would be a great ruler. Being the youngest in his family, Joseph was loved more than all the other children by his father, Israel, and this was a very difficult pill for his brothers to swallow. The first dream that Joseph had was that he would rule over his brothers, his father and his mother, and his family was not impressed with his dream (see Genesis 37:5-10). Joseph's brothers sold him as a slave to Midianite traders who took him to Egypt and finally sold him to Potiphar, an officer of Pharoah and captain of the guard. Joseph was a successful man in Potiphar's house and found favor in the sight of his master, so much so that Potiphar left Joseph to oversee all that he had. However, Potiphar's wife wrongfully accused Joseph of trying to sleep with her, and Potiphar was so angry that he threw Joseph into prison.

However, God was with Joseph, even in prison, and Joseph again found favor. Joseph was then put in charge of all the prisoners. It was during this time that Pharaoh's butler and baker had offended

Pharoah, and they were thrown into the same prison as Joseph and put under his guard. While in prison, the butler and the baker had dreams that they were very worried about. When Joseph saw their worry, he asked the butler and baker to share their dreams with him, and he would consult with God on their meanings. God gave Joseph the interpretations, and Joseph shared these with both men. Joseph also asked the butler to remember him when he was restored as the butler to Pharaoh.

However, the butler forgot Joseph. Two years passed before Pharaoh also had a dream that troubled him, and he called for his magicians and wise men to interpret his dream, but no one could. It was then that the butler remembered what Joseph had done for him, and he shared this with Pharaoh. Pharaoh called immediately for Joseph. Joseph was summoned, cleaned up and presented to Pharaoh. God gave Joseph the interpretation of Pharaoh's dream. The land of Egypt was going to have seven years of plenty that would be followed by seven years of famine. Joseph also advised Pharaoh to choose a wise leader to save and store enough food during the seven good years to see them through the seven years of famine. Pharaoh was so impressed with Joseph's interpretation that he chose Joseph to be the wise leader, and he put him in charge of all his land: "You shall be over my house, and all my people shall be ruled according to your word; only in regard to the throne will I be greater than you. . . . See, I have set you over all the land of Egypt" (Genesis 41:40-41, NKJV).

Joseph achieved his dream of being a great ruler, but he needed two types of people in his life to help him—a butler and a baker. They played instrumental roles in Joseph's realizing his dream. Why?

- *Butlers* will open the door for your dreams. Not only will they open the door, but they will also announce you to the world.
- *Bakers* will take all the ingredients in your life and combine them for you to achieve your dream. All the ingredients, if eaten on their own, don't taste good (like the raw eggs, flour and sugar), but when they're put together in the right way, they will make a great cake for everyone to enjoy.

Mentors act as these butlers and bakers in your life. They are people who have been there, done that and gotten the t-shirt. They are people who are farther ahead in life but are willing to help you navigate the pitfalls in your own journey.

SELECTING YOUR MENTORS

There are certain key attributes that you should be looking for when selecting your mentors. Good mentors have a willingness to share skills, knowledge and expertise. They should also be able to identify the current stage of your journey. Good mentors can remember what it was like starting out in the field, so they can provide insightful guidance and constructive feedback. They should be role models who demonstrate positive attitudes and take personal interest in seeing you succeed.

My good friend, Jeffrey Smith, a pastor and leadership consultant in Virginia, once taught on the list of attributes of people you want in your life. He says that you want mentors who . . .

- are not afraid of obstacles,
- don't just want to blend in with the crowd,
- are not intimidated by your problem,

- work well with others in your life,
- are creative,
- move you towards your faith in God,
- know how to go up,
- have faith and
- have breakthrough in them.

You *WILL* need mentors to succeed! Whom do you have in your life right now acting as a mentor? I encourage you to begin searching for some who will come alongside you on your journey to become a great leader of tomorrow. My challenge to you is to *surround yourself with the right mentors, so that you can see your dreams soar to unimaginable levels.* Right now, take out a pen and piece of paper, and start writing down a list of potential mentors whom you believe you should have in your life.

Warren Buffett says, "If you want to soar like an eagle in life, you can't be flocking with the turkeys." I like to say, "If you want to fly with eagles, get rid of the turkeys in your life." Selecting the right eagles to mentor you along your journey can be the difference between staying on the ground or flying high above the clouds and the crowds.

Sometimes along this road of preparing you will feel lost, you will feel like you should be further along in your journey and you will feel like it is taking too long to happen. This is the time you need to continue to press on and keep preparing. The journey in preparing is most often longer than the actual task or assignment that you have been called to fulfill. But preparation time is never wasted. Remember Abraham Lincoln when he said, "Give me six hours to chop down a tree, and I will spend the first four sharpening the axe"?

You need to prepare well to lead well.

CHAPTER 3

PREPARING YOURSELF AND YOUR SIGNIFICANT OTHERS

ontinuing on from the previous chapter, let's keep looking at the first letter in the acronym **PILOT**—the **P** for **P**reparing. In this chapter, I want to get more personal.

I have come to the realization that a leader's journey cannot only be about preparing him or herself. For a leader's journey to be successful, the process of preparing will also need to extend to certain significant others, the people closest to the leader, which in most cases will mean the leader's family. Preparing yourself and your significant others is a necessary and vital step to ensure success for the journey that lies ahead.

In this chapter, I will begin by reviewing the importance for leaders in preparing themselves and those closest to them, and secondly the importance of preparing for the pain of leading because there will be pain in this journey. These two aspects are so crucial for the success for any future leader that if neglected, will certainly hinder you from finishing well, or worse, stop you from even finishing at all.

PREPARING YOUR FAMILY AND HEALTH

Leaders need to ensure that they are not only preparing themselves for the journey but also their families and health. The following scenario was presented to me while I attended a session at the Partner Assessment Centre—a key process we had to go through in qualifying to becoming a partner or director at Deloitte:

> *There is a critical issue with one of your largest clients, and they require an urgent meeting with you at 8am the next day. It is your biggest account, and you stand the risk of losing it. Your daughter's music recital is the next day also at 8am. You have a choice to make.*

As a young man in my early thirties, who did not fully understand my WHO yet, the answer was a no-brainer—the client took priority. Why? Because that was the answer I thought they wanted to hear! Interestingly, these scenarios weren't so much about the answers we gave, but the explanations we provided for our answers. The Assessment Centre was essentially testing me to see if I fully understood my WHO. Most of my colleagues gave a similar answer because we thought that was what Deloitte wanted to hear.

A HEALTHY HOME AND A HEALTHY BODY WILL GET YOU THERE.

A Healthy Home and Body

Another key module we focus on in our **PILOT** program concludes: "A healthy home and a healthy body will get you there." Isn't it ironic that in our busy lives we're unable to take the necessary time to look after our families or health, but as soon as there is an urgent family or health crisis we're immediately able to attend to it? Or is this just me? Why is it always easier to move things around to attend to a crisis, yet we can't move things around for our kids' school plays, swimming galas or annual physical check-ups?

Wheel of Life

Most of our lives can be broken down into several areas as illustrated in the "Wheel of Life" diagram below.

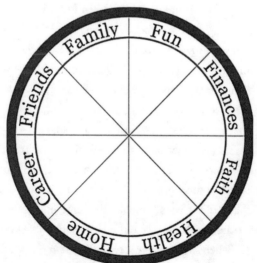

Figure 2: Wheel of Life—Synergy Strategies

In a perfect world, you'd want this wheel to be fully aligned all the time. But, like a tire on a car, the more you use the wheel, the more it begins to lose alignment. While it's not necessary to keep all of these areas *perfectly* in sync all the time, it's important to constantly check your alignment before something tragic happens. In your journey, there will often be seasons where you require much more focus in a selected area than the other areas of your wheel of life. Sometimes you'll require more family time, sometimes you'll have more time for a gym workout and sometimes you'll be more occupied with work and travel. There will be times, when unplanned or unexpected life events may require you to shift your focus, like a family tragedy or a bad doctor's report. The key is to *recognize*, *understand* and *manage* those seasons without feeling shamed or guilty.

There were many times in my life when I didn't recognize, understand and manage these seasons. This is evident in the difference in my relationships with my two daughters. My eldest, Arianna, was born in 2006 during the height of my Deloitte career when I was striving towards becoming a partner, traveling extensively and working long hours to advance my career. I wasn't at home much, and I missed many of Arianna's milestones. So Arianna had, and sometimes still has, what I can best refer to as a nervous relationship with me. She never truly knows how I'm going to respond. On the other hand, Alessandra (Alex) was born in 2010 when I'd grown up a little more as a leader and didn't want to make the same mistakes. I definitely overcompensated with Alex, so our relationship is *a lot* more relaxed. Often times, when she gives me a *piece of her young mind*, I realize it's a little too relaxed for my liking!

I have now learned through many painful lessons that life is all about family. More so, I believe God is all about family, and He's looking for families to honor Him. God's plan to redeem the world began with one home, one family—which was the family of the patriarch Abraham as documented in the Bible. Your family doesn't just need your money or possessions, it needs you. I believe that our families come before any position or title and even before any calling God has on our lives.

Faith, Family and Fitness

Faith, family and fitness (your health) are the most important things you need to prepare well for. Without faith, you have no hope. Without your family, no matter how great your life seems to the world, it will be worthless to you in the end. Without your health, your journey may finish much quicker than it ought to. These are painful lessons I've learned and continue to learn. The challenge with your faith, family and fitness is that when they break, they're not easily repaired. The below extract was written by Brian Dyson, CEO of Coca-Cola from 1988 until 1994:

> Imagine life as a game in which you are juggling some five balls in the air. You name them—Work—Family—Health–Friends—Spirit, and you're keeping all of these in the air. You will soon understand that work is a rubber ball. If you drop it, it will bounce back. But the other four balls—family, health, friends and spirit (or faith) are made of glass. If you drop one of these, they will be irrevocably scuffed, marked, nicked, damaged

*or even shattered. They will never be the same. You must under-
stand that and strive for balance in your life.*

The one ball I'm working really hard on right now is my fitness and
health. While I wish I worked on this earlier in my life, I'm glad I've
finally *recognized* and *understood* it's importance. Now I'm trying to
manage it while I still can. There have been many warning signs over
the years, but I simply chose to ignore them as my health didn't seem
important. Your health may be a silent killer that could eventually
derail your leadership journey. One simple way that I have learned to
manage my health is a compulsory annual medical check-up because
what I can't measure, I can't manage. Every leader should make this
a priority and never skip this important annual event. This will allow
him or her to take any necessary steps to improve the areas that
require improvement.

The more *should haves* in a person's life, the less *happiness*. I *should
have* taken better care of my health. I *should have* attended my child's
awards evening. I *should have* told my wife I loved her more. I *should
have* spent more time with my family. To adopt a phrase from Brenda
Chand, "Don't let anyone *should have* on you."

PREPARING FOR THE PAIN OF LEADING

Preparing for the pain of leading isn't a topic many of us want to talk
about or even consider. I felt the same until I read Dr. Chand's book
Leadership Pain. Get a copy; it'll be a source of encouragement and
support when you experience the pain awaiting you as you grow into
an integral leader of tomorrow.

At the time of writing, the world and its leaders were grappling with the greatest global pandemic in the previous one hundred years. Many were dealing with unprecedented pain, and I'm sure many of them were not taught how to deal with it. I came across a beautiful poem written by Claire Lagerwall entitled *Mr. President, You're Tired*. It touched on the pain our South African president, Cyril Ramaphosa, was going through in managing the COVID-19 pandemic:

My President, you're tired
We can see it in your eyes
It's not really something
You can easily hide
We see you across
Our television screens
Addressing the nation
On a history unseen
We see you stumble
Over words being said
And I pause to wonder
What's going on in your head
Are you coping, Sir
With all that you face
A broken nation
Looking to you for grace
Are you okay, Mr. President
You look so sad
Your eyes tell a story
I'm sorry it's so bad

We pray for you
Hold you in our thoughts
This is a war
We have never fought
I'm glad that you're ours
That we don't have to share
That our precious nation
Is under your care
With our cries of faith
We trusted God for a man
Who could steer a nation
Into unknown lands
Thank you, my President
For being so brave
Whilst a nation is judging
Each move that you've made
We pray for you Sir
We really do
And we thank God
For a leader like you

PAIN IS NECESSARY

In *Leadership Pain*, Dr. Chand presents two key principles on the pain of leading:

1) You can only grow to the threshold of your pain.

The more pain you're willing to bear, the more you will grow. When leaders say, "That's enough," while there is nothing wrong with this, they must realize that this will be the limit of their growth. This concept is similar to Dr. John Maxwell's "Law of the Lid," which the story of David versus Goliath demonstrates. A giant named Goliath mocked the armies of Israel. They were terrified of Goliath, so they didn't want to fight him. Saul, who was the king at the time, was an experienced soldier, and "he was taller than any of the people from his shoulders upward" (1 Samuel 10:23, ESV). Yet Saul was also fearful of Goliath, and this paralyzed him from leading his army—Saul had reached his "lid." David, on the other hand, reviewed the situation, carefully selected his weapon (a sling and five stones) and defeated the giant. The difference between Saul and David was that Saul had reached the threshold of his pain, so that was as much as he grew. David took over from Saul as the king from that point, and his success far exceeded his predecessor.

I always like comparing the role of the CEO of a small-sized company to the CEO of a major global company. What is the difference? It is the amount of *pain* they are carrying. The more pain you are willing to bear, the more you will grow.

THE MORE PAIN YOU ARE WILLING TO BEAR, THE MORE YOU WILL GROW.

A formula for PAIN is as follows:

GROWTH = CHANGE

CHANGE = LOSS

LOSS = PAIN

Therefore, GROWTH = PAIN

2) Future leaders who want to grow will require some sort of change.

Change is difficult for most people and will lead to some losses, which are painful. So if we're preparing to grow in our leadership abilities, then we must be preparing for the pain that will accompany this growth.

I've been traveling since my early twenties, and I can recount many painful stories of being alone in foreign countries—unable to speak the language, too shy to order something to eat and working in environments with very different people. The worst I experience is from being away from my wife and daughters. In the early years, we didn't have mobile phones or Skype or WhatsApp, so I couldn't talk to my wife whenever I wanted. I remember my first long period away from her back in 2000 when I was seconded to Deloitte in Atlanta. I'd bought a calling card, but because the cost to call was very high per minute, I could only really call Kirbashnee once a week for a few minutes at most. I used to count the days and hours until our next call. It was painful, but I was growing. I didn't realize it, but it was preparing me for my future role. Seasoned travelers know that traveling can be daunting. I know now that those many years of traveling to all parts of the world, and being able to grow through the many painful experiences, has prepared me well for this next stage in my life.

My first truly painful travel experience was on that working assignment to Atlanta. Kirbashnee and I had been married for only a month when I had to pack my bags to go away for close to six months. I left my hometown of Durban to take a forty-five minute flight to Johannesburg and then a connecting flight to Atlanta. I recall breaking down in tears when I arrived in Johannesburg as I realized I was going to be away from Kirbashnee for so long. I felt lonely and scared, and I didn't want to make the trip anymore. I remember calling her from Johannesburg and telling her that she needed to get on the next flight to Atlanta, no matter the cost. She must have thought I was crazy, but that was the pain I was going through. Fastforward twenty years, and Atlanta has become a central and familiar point of contact linking me to many friends.

What if I had chosen not to endure the pain of that first trip to Atlanta? I wouldn't have grown to where I am today. I knew that if I wanted to grow in my career, it required a change. That change was an opportunity to work abroad. It came with much loss as I spent precious time away from the woman I loved in the early stages of our marriage. It was indeed painful, but I'm so glad I endured it because it prepared me for what I do now—travel regularly all over the world to meet new people, work in many different countries and engage with many cultures. Growth will require you to go through change. To change means you will lose something, and that loss is always going to be painful. But if you want to grow, you'll have to go through it. I know the pain is real, but the promise is of a greater reality.

I KNOW THE PAIN IS REAL, BUT THE PROMISE IS OF A GREATER REALITY.

CHOOSE TO BELIEVE THE PROMISE OVER THE PAIN

As you embark on your journey, you need to hold on to the promise over your life. This promise is what you know you want to achieve. We all have a promise. We just need to find it and hold on to it to achieve it.

During your stage of preparing, you'll start to understand *WHO* you are, and you'll begin understanding and creating the vision for your life. You know where you are and where you are headed, but it is in the middle where most future leaders throw in the towel. Why? Because they experience pain and don't know what to do. Even as I'm writing this book, I'm going through a season of extended pain—*the middle period*. I can best describe this experience as being three days from nowhere—*I know where I came from, I know where I am going, but right now I feel stuck in the middle.* It's during this middle period where you need to push through and not quit. It's the leadership pain that, as a future leader, you need to overcome to get to the promise.

- You need to push through the pain you are in right now.
- You need to push through the intense pressures, scrutiny and hard work that you're experiencing, which are part of your continual developmental process.

- You need to push through the self-doubts that constantly swirl in your head saying that you're on the wrong path.
- You need to push through the daily routine. You're expecting great things to happen any day, but life continues its same day-after-day routine.

In this middle period, I've needed to find something to hold on to during this time. In my search, I found a few golden nuggets, which I'd like to share with you.

First, I'm choosing to believe the promise that I'll achieve my desired end and my purpose in life as a leader, even when the facts scream, "There's no way you're going to get there!" As a spiritual person, I believe that God has given each one of us a promise or purpose in life, and if we stick to it, we'll achieve this promise. Remember Joseph, the great grandson of the Jewish patriarch Abraham. Joseph didn't consider his current circumstances as final. When he was thrown into the pit by his brothers, the facts screamed, "There's no way!" But he believed the promise that he would be the greatest in his family. When he was sold as a slave to the Ishmaelites, the facts screamed, "There's no way!" But he believed the promise in his dream. When he was thrown into prison, the facts screamed, "There's no way!" But he still believed the promise.

When you're in this middle period of your life as a future leader, you need to make a choice to hold on to the promise in your heart, regardless of how the process looks. Don't give up on your future because of failures in the past or weaknesses in the present. Hold on to the promise because what you hold on to will hold onto you!

HOLD ON TO THE PROMISE BECAUSE WHAT YOU HOLD ON TO WILL HOLD ONTO YOU!

Secondly, I'm learning to activate the P³ principle: Patience + Perseverance = Promise.

A Christian's life is sometimes characterized in the Bible as a *race to be run* and a *struggle to be fought*. Other prominent terms used of the Christian's life are *labor*, *toil* or *work*. As a future leader, you'll realize that it's not going to be easy. You'll indeed have struggles, trials and hardships. This is where you need patience and perseverance.

Patience refers to the quality of enduring pain, hardship, provocation or annoyance with calmness. It can also refer to a calm willingness to tolerate delay. I've learned that there are three aspects to patience: (1) Patience never gives into negative or demanding circumstances, (2) Patience involves coping with difficult people, and (3) For a Christian person, patience accepts God's plan for everything.

Working with many talented future leaders, the one thing I regularly notice is their lack of patience in getting to their goal or promise. They want it now, and they want it quickly. They don't believe in the process they need to go through.

The *American Heritage Dictionary* defines perseverance as: "steady persistence in adhering to a course of action, a belief, or a purpose; steadfastness."

The Olympic Creed or guiding principles of the modern Olympic Games, is a quote by Pierre de Coubertin. He got the idea for this phrase from a speech given by Bishop Ethelbert Talbot at a service for Olympic champions during the 1908 Olympic Games and slightly adapted it to read thus: "The most important thing in the Olympic Games is not to win but to take part, just as the most important thing in life is not the triumph but the struggle. The essential thing is not to have conquered but to have fought well."

The third nugget is a word called hope. Joyce Meyer, American host of the television show *Enjoying Everyday Life*, often talks about how she used to be the most negative person she'd ever met. Her motto was: "If I don't expect anything good to happen, then I won't be disappointed when it doesn't." One definition of hope is "a favorable and confident expectation." It's a positive attitude and the happy anticipation that something good is going to happen. Once mankind loses hope, it loses everything. Pain is real, but so is hope. It changes things. Your hopes, not your pains, should shape your future. Anne Lamott concurs, "Hope begins in the dark, the stubborn hope that if you just show up and try to do the right thing, the dawn will come. You wait and watch and work; you don't give up."

Like my favorite biblical character Joseph, I *don't want to be distracted* by the pain that will keep me away from my end. Joseph held on to the promise, and the promise held on to him. If Joseph can do it, then so can we! In fact, we possess a distinct advantage over Joseph— we've got his story, and the stories of other great leaders, that we can learn from. They remind and caution us about the need to prepare for pain, and they help us get through it. We need to remember that diamonds don't sparkle until they're cut, roses don't release fragrance until they're crushed and stars don't shine until the darkest night.

Pain is a natural part of preparing be integral leaders of tomorrow. Let the promise of your desired goals shape you and make you.

LET THE PROMISE OF YOUR DESIRED GOALS SHAPE YOU AND MAKE YOU.

PREPARING WELL CONTINUOUSLY

If you picked up this book, I'm guessing you have a BIG dream and you want to live a meaningful and purposeful life. Whether you're a future leader just starting out on your journey or you're an experienced leader still on the journey, I hope you're realizing that you need to be preparing well continuously to achieve future success. If you fail to prepare, be prepared to fail.

The challenge for leaders is that this process of *preparing* is an ongoing cycle. It never stops and it's not once-off. The measure of your continual preparation will determine the measure of your success. It was the famous King Solomon who said, "Diligence is one's most important possession" (Proverbs 12:27, ISV). The continuous process of preparing will require diligence because the process of *preparing* is rarely straightforward. You'll continuously experience both highs and lows. Many people only look at Joseph as being the second in charge of the land, and don't realize that he had a cycle of continual preparation. Joseph went from the pit to the palace, from the palace to the prison, and from the prison to his promise (the 4 Ps—pit, palace, prison and promise).

I pray that you'll have loads of palace experiences, but you'll need to be diligent through your seasons in the pit and the prison. It'll be in these seasons that you will be preparing and equipping yourself for the palaces that will come into your life.

Madiba, in his Rivonia Trial speech in 1964 during one of his pit and prison seasons, penned one of his most famous speeches. This extract perfectly sums up the diligence you'll need during your seasons of preparing:

I have fought against white domination, and I have fought against black domination. I have cherished the ideal of a democratic and free society in which all persons will live together in harmony and with equal opportunities. It is an ideal which I hope to live for and to see realized. But if it needs be, it is an ideal for which I am prepared to die.

Preparing well, continuously and diligently will determine the measure of your success as a future leader. So take heed to prepare yourself and your significant others as you continue onward.

CHAPTER 4

IF YOU HAVE INTEGRITY, YOU HAVE EVERYTHING

With integrity, you have nothing to fear, since you have nothing to hide.
With integrity, you will do the right thing, so you will have no guilt.
—Zig Ziglar

et's look at the second letter in the acronym **PILOT**—I for Integral. When I talk about *integral*, I'm simply referring to integrity. Integrity is probably one of the most overused—yet, at the same time most misunderstood—words that leaders throw about today. I literally mean throw about, as if integrity is a rubber ball that can be bounced around or thrown up in the air—caught when one feels like it or dropped when life gets too difficult.

Integrity is a word that is often boldly and proudly emblazoned as a core value of most large global corporations, yet we continue to have major corporate scandals. Scandals that cause innocent people to lose their hard-earned money. At the time of writing, South Africa had recently been rocked by some of the largest corporate scandals in the country's history involving companies such as Steinhoff, KPMG and African Bank. Even my beloved Deloitte, the organization I was part of for fourteen years of my early career, has had its share of controversy!

Many questions were asked: "How could these leaders have done such things?" "How did they do this for so long, and no one knew about it?" and "Where was the corporate governance in these large organizations?" However, the one question not being asked, which is in the hearts and minds of the millions of people who have suffered as a result of these corporate scandals, is this: "How could you have done this to me? I trusted you." This is a question I pray you never get asked or faced with during your lifetime of leading. For years to come, people will continue to question the integrity of these companies and their leaders. But what do we mean when we speak of integrity?

HOW COULD YOU HAVE DONE THIS TO ME? I TRUSTED YOU.

WHAT IS INTEGRITY?

My first real introspection of the word "integrity" was during 2006 to 2007. I was thirty years old and preparing for my leadership assessment at Deloitte. Being a partner in one of the big four global audit and advisory firms would be a high point in my career, especially for an ordinary kid like me who grew up in a little Indian community.

It may have been a pipe dream when I first started my career in 1998 as an article clerk, but now it was serious stuff. A partner was the epitome of a perfect leader to me. Partners and directors were successful, honest, reliable, highly respected and trustworthy. They possessed an almost god-like presence and character. Never in my wildest imagination did I think that I could achieve this position and gain this title in my lifetime. It was through God's providence that I stood at the door. If I got through the assessment, then I was on my way to a good measure of success in my corporate career.

But during the assessment, I did something really stupid!

I was required to write a paper on a topic of my choice and then present it to the assessment panel. Most of my peers prepared papers on technical aspects of accounting or auditing, but not I. Mr. Wise Guy decided to write a paper called, "My Pillars of Leadership." I presented what I believed were the right pillars of leadership as a future Deloitte leader. I also ranked myself up against these pillars, highlighted where my challenges lay and discussed how I could apply these pillars to make a valuable contribution. Many an aspiring young leader reading this book might be thinking, *Wow, that's a great paper to present!* I thought so too at the time. But it was like I walked into my own planned show on Comedy Central: *The Roasting of Nicholas John.* For the next two days, the assessment panel, which was made up of several senior partners and a few professional psychologists, tore me apart over my naivety and lack of experiential insights on my topic. It was easy for me to write about these things from a theoretical stand-point, but did I really know what I was talking about? Fortunately, my story ends well. I was still admitted into the partnership in June 2007.

However, as I sit here nearly thirteen years later on in my professional career, I'm grateful for the risk I took on my paper. The pillars of leadership I presented back then were integrity, excellence, strategic vision and personal responsibility. It was my first real analysis of integrity as a value, even though I didn't know much about it back then. Now, let me try to unpack four definitions of integrity that I've learned by leading through the hard knocks of life.

INCORRUPTIBILITY, SOUNDNESS, COMPLETENESS AND WHOLENESS

The first definition of integrity is directly from the dictionary. According to the *Merriam-Webster Dictionary*, integrity can be defined as follows:

> *A firm adherence to a code of especially moral or artistic values—INCORRUPTIBILTY. An unimpaired condition— SOUNDNESS. The quality or state of being complete or undivided—COMPLETENESS. Integer—WHOLENESS*

Integrity evolved from the Latin adjective *integer*, meaning whole or complete. It's where we get the term whole number, which we learned at school. In this context, integrity is the inner sense of wholeness derived from qualities like honesty and consistency of character. In summary, integrity is a state of being incorruptible, a state of being sound in mind, body, spirit and soul, a state of being complete and a state of being whole.

HONESTY, RELIABILITY, CONSISTENCY AND CONFIDENTIALITY

In the second definition, integrity can be defined as a person who is honest, reliable, consistent *and* confidential. Notice that there is an "and" not an "or" in this definition. It requires a person to possess *all* of these qualities. I learned this definition of integrity a few years back while on a "Good to Great" training program based on the book by Jim Collins. Let's take a closer look at this definition:

- Honesty—the quality of being honest, which means that a person is free of deceit; is sincere and truthful; is morally correct or virtuous

- Reliability—the quality of being reliable, which means a person who is consistently good in quality or performance; able to be trusted

- Consistency—the quality of being consistent, which means a person is unchanging in nature, standard or effect over time; is acting or doing in the same way over time, especially so as to be fair or accurate

- Confidentiality—the quality of being a confidential person, which means things that are intended to be kept secret are kept secret

TO WALK RIGHTLY OR UPRIGHTLY

The third definition of integrity comes from the word "righteousness" which means to walk rightly or uprightly. Growing up in a pastor's home as a PK (pastor's kid), it would be remiss of me to exclude this impactful definition. As a Christian leader, one of the key definitions of integrity can be linked to being a righteous person or a person walking rightly in the sight of God. Righteous can be defined as being morally right or justifiable, and righteousness can be defined as the *quality* of being morally right or justifiable. A biblically based definition of righteousness involves being in right standing with God. Furthermore, I'd add that being in right standing with God is where your heart is beating in the same rhythm as God's. It means that you're living out God's will, purpose and heart for your life.

For Christian leaders, God makes it clear that keeping His commandments (or being in right standing with Him) is the essence of integrity. The high principles of honesty and good character manifested in a man or woman of integrity come from adherence to divine principles. We need to realize that true righteousness is only found in God, and as we grow closer to God, the clearer the picture of righteousness becomes to us. As you continue developing a deeper relationship with God, you will develop a deeper understanding of what true righteousness means and what you need to do to continue developing in righteousness.

King Solomon in the Bible committed himself to serving God, and the keeping of God's law was an integral part of that commitment. That is why he penned such famous proverbs on integrity and walking in righteousness as these quoted using the New International Version of the Bible:

- "The path of the righteous is like the morning sun, shining ever brighter till the full light of day." (Proverbs 4:18)
- "Blessings crown the head of the righteous. . . ." (Proverbs 10:6)

- "The mouth of the righteous is a fountain of life. . . ." (Proverbs 10:11)
- "The tongue of the righteous is choice silver. . . ." (Proverbs 10:20)
- "The lips of the righteous nourish many. . . ." (Proverbs 10:21)
- ". . . The righteous stand firm forever." (Proverbs 10:25)
- "The righteous will never be uprooted. . . ." (Proverbs 10:30)
- "The house of the righteous contains great treasure. . . ." (Proverbs 15:6)
- "The heart of the righteous weighs its answers. . . ." (Proverbs 15:28)
- ". . . For a throne is established through righteousness." (Proverbs 16:12)
- "The righteous lead blameless lives. . . ." (Proverbs 20:7)
- "From the mouth of the righteous comes the fruit of wisdom. . . ." (Proverbs 10:31)
- "Truly the righteous attain life. . . ." (Proverbs 11:19)
- "The desire of the righteous ends only in good. . . ." (Proverbs 11:23)
- "The fruit of the righteous is a tree of life. . . ." (Proverbs 11:30)
- "The plans of the righteous are just. . . ." (Proverbs 12:5)
- "The righteous choose their friends carefully. . . ." (Proverbs 12:26)
- "The righteous hate what is false. . . ." (Proverbs 13:5)

- "The light of the righteous shines brightly. . . ."
  (Proverbs 13:9)
- "Righteousness exalts a nation. . . ." (Proverbs 14:34)
- ". . . But the righteous are as bold as a lion." (Proverbs 28:1)
- "The righteous care about justice for the poor. . . ."
  (Proverbs 29:7)
- "The righteous detest the dishonest. . . ." Proverbs 29:27

It's sad, though, that this great king didn't walk with integrity all the days of his life. He made many mistakes, like we will do. Nevertheless, Solomon still gave us good advice on the subject of integrity when he said, "The integrity of the upright guides them. . . ." in Proverbs 11:3 (NIV), "Righteousness guards the man of integrity. . . ." in Proverbs 13:6 (NIV) and "Whoever walks in integrity walks securely. . . ." in Proverbs 10:9 (NIV). Therefore, walking rightly is akin to being an integral person. Integrity and righteousness are not mutually inclusive.

DOING THE RIGHT THINGS WHEN NO ONE IS WATCHING

This last definition of integrity is one that is closest to me, as it's the one we adopt and teach at LeaderGrow. It's also C. S. Lewis's definition: "Integrity is doing the right things when no one is watching."

INTEGRITY IS DOING THE RIGHT THINGS WHEN NO ONE IS WATCHING. —C. S. LEWIS

I learned this definition from my current organization, and it was taught to me by our former chairman, Arnold Vermaak. It's easy to do the right things when everyone is watching, but what about the times when no one is watching or when it's just you? It's the one definition that pierced me deeply because it spoke volumes about me as a person and where I was on my journey towards integral leadership.

Can I be real with you? I mentioned that I was roasted by the panel at my Deloitte leadership assessment, and the real reason was that I was talking about stuff (mostly integrity) that sounded right and made me feel good about myself, but I had no clue what it meant to be an integral person or to have integrity in leading. While the panel gave me lots of positive and negative feedback during the process, there is one comment that will stay with me for the rest of my life—"He can talk the talk, but can he walk the walk?" Is this not similar to most leaders today?

HE CAN TALK THE TALK, BUT CAN HE WALK THE WALK?

I've now learned that integrity is a quality you can't fake. For years, I was faking it. I could certainly talk the talk about integrity, but I wasn't walking the walk or walking the talk. Deep down I knew that I was nowhere close to being an integral person; I wasn't really leading with integrity. In fact, I was very far from it. I was living a lie in front of my family, church leaders and the many organizations I worked for. I was just paying lip service to them. I wanted to look like and be perceived as an integral person, but I was just continuing to be my normal selfish self. But there was always a genuine, heartfelt desire to be a person of integrity. So, my journey towards integrity continues as I come to understand WHO I am as a person and leader because WHAT I do (my outside) will always flow from WHO I am (my inside).

WHY IS INTEGRITY IMPORTANT IN LEADERS?

What's all the fuss about integrity? Why do leaders need to be integral, and why should they be leading with integrity? Having integrity as a leader is vital, if not most important. Let me recap on the quote by the late Dr. Myles Munroe in his book *The Spirit of Leadership*: "The number one need all over the globe today, is not money, social programs or even new governments. It is quality, moral, disciplined, principle-centered leadership."

The world is looking for "quality, moral, disciplined, principle-centered leadership." True leaders know that integrity is the foundation of their leadership—they stand up for what they believe in and never compromise by cheating. Here are the key reasons why integrity is so important for a leader.

Leaders with integrity know WHO they are.

Leaders with integrity understand their *WHO* (their heart and their purpose), so what they do will consistently flow from WHO they are. They listen to their hearts and do the right thing. Their actions are open for everyone to see and their followers feel safe and secure knowing that all leadership decisions are principled.

Integrity helps leaders restore glory.

The world is looking for leaders to restore glory—to their nations, countries, states, governments, health care, educational institutions and every other facet of society. Most importantly, the world *needs* leaders to restore glory in homes and families. What do I mean by "restore glory?" Well, the definitions of glory are (1) high renown or honor, (2) magnificence or great beauty and (3) a state of gratification or exaltation. Is that not what we all desire in every area of our lives? I've had countless experiences where leaders have failed by bringing anything *but* glory, and their leadership has turned out to be one big fake show. Integrity cannot be faked.

Let me use another personal example. I'm exceptionally proud to have worked at Deloitte for the first fourteen years of my career. I have wonderful and happy memories working for such a prestigious global brand with respected values, fantastic people and an enviable client base. Deloitte has all the trimmings to make an employee feel honored and gratified to be associated with them. It was a state of glory for me, and the leaders were doing something right for me to have felt that way.

Future leaders who want to lead with genuine integrity need to be aware of these things when it comes to restoring glory:

- The glory is never about you! You are there as a leader to bring glory to the people and the cause.

- The Hebrew word *Ichabod* means "the glory has departed." You could be leading an organization whose glory has long departed, and you are operating with fake glory.
- The Hebrew word *kabod* means "heavy glory," which is what every leader should aspire to. It's the genuine glory that permeates your organization and delights your people.

Integrity is the key required to attain glory, which is why people are looking for genuine integrity in their leaders.

Leaders with integrity understand that character counts.

Your character matters. D. L. Moody once said, "Character is what you are in the dark." How a leader deals with the circumstances of life says a lot about his or her character.

THE DEVELOPMENT OF CHARACTER IS AT THE HEART OF LEADERSHIP.

In *The Maxwell Leadership Bible*, John Maxwell states that "Crisis doesn't necessarily mold character, but it certainly does reveal it. Adversity is a crossroads that makes a person choose one of two paths: character or compromise." Leaders compromise so much in these present times. Every time leaders choose character, they become stronger, even if that choice brings negative consequences. The development of character is at the heart of leadership. Character is more than talk, and it's more than having talent and ability. Talent is a gift, but character is a choice. Talent and ability will only take you so far, but character brings lasting success for people.

Leaders with integrity gain the trust of people.

Trust is the essence of any relationship in life. When we operate from integrity, we gain the trust of other people. Most importantly, we gain the trust of the people we're leading. If your team sees you as principled, dependable and fair in your actions, then trust develops. When there is trust, people feel safe in your presence, and you gain influence, which allows you to lead more effectively. There is nothing worse than working with a person—especially a leader—that you cannot trust. Once trust in a leader is broken, it's almost impossible to regain.

LEADERS WITH INTEGRITY AREN'T AFRAID OF REALITY. —BRIAN TRACY

Leaders with integrity aren't afraid to face the truth.

This is called the reality principle or "seeing the world as it really is, not as you wish it to be." I read an article, "The Importance of Honesty and Integrity in Business," written by Brian Tracy who said:

> *Leaders with integrity aren't afraid of reality. It is perhaps the most important principle of leadership and dependent on integrity because it demands truthfulness and honesty. Many companies and organizations fail because they don't follow the reality principle. Integrity means telling the truth even if the truth is*

ugly. Better to be honest than to delude others, because then you are probably deluding yourself, too. Leaders need to be courageous, but they also need to be open to the idea that they could be wrong. There are many leaders who eventually fail because they refuse to question their own assumptions or conclusions.

The coronavirus that the world is dealing with has revealed the integrity of many world leaders. Some leaders were afraid of the reality of the global pandemic and the loss of human lives. Other leaders lead with genuine integrity and weren't afraid to be open about the reality of the pandemic. They were honest with their people, so their people have trusted them even more to lead them through the horrible crisis.

Leaders with integrity are role models for future leaders.

Leaders with integrity become role models whether they like it or not. Integrity is the most vital element required for principle-centered leadership in future leaders. Corporations, employees, customers, churches, communities and families want leaders they can trust. When you demonstrate integrity, you show everyone that you can be trusted and respected. Integral leaders will develop more integral leaders. King Solomon in Proverbs 11:4 (NIV) wrote, "A thick bankroll is no help when life falls apart, but a principled life can stand up to the worst."

A THICK BANKROLL IS NO HELP WHEN LIFE FALLS APART, BUT A PRINCIPLED LIFE CAN STAND UP TO THE WORST. —PROVERBS 11:4 (MSG)

THE INTEGRITY TEST

It's time for us to take a quick integrity test. Please review and honestly answer these five questions:

1) Do I give a full day's work for a full day's pay?
2) Am I honest regarding my travel claims and expenses?
3) Do I avoid misusing office facilities?
4) Do I pay all my traffic fines timely and through the appropriate channels?
5) Am I always truthful when completing my tax returns?

Give yourself a point for each yes. How many did you score out of five?

We use this light-hearted test during our **PILOT** programs, but, in its simplicity, it powerfully demonstrates how we often misconstrue what integrity really is. It reveals how we can sometimes compartmentalize our lives when it comes to integrity.

INTEGRITY IS INTEGRITY

I've experienced, even in myself, how easy it is to compartmentalize our lives when it comes to integrity. But the integrity test makes a simple point—integrity is integrity. There aren't different types of integrity, and there aren't different compartments in your life that allow you to switch your integrity on or off when you need to or when it's convenient.

Let's look at a practical example from my experience working in the global corporate arena:

You are the chief financial officer (CFO) of a global organization that is listed on both the New York and London stock exchanges.

> *Thousands of investors look to you as the main gatekeeper of their investments, and you are highly regarded as a man of integrity when it comes to your job. You have just presented the annual financial statements at an AGM, and investors are really proud of the results of the company for the past year. Very satisfied, you settle into your hotel for the evening with a rather attractive young woman, who is not your wife. Funny coincidence is that you bump into your biggest shareholder in the hotel lobby at the same time that you are in an affectionate, yet rather embarrassing, embrace with your attractive young woman friend.*

If I'm the biggest shareholder, how do you explain to me that I can trust you with our multibillion dollar investments when you may be cheating on your wife? "That's easy," you may say, "I would never cheat at the office!" I've heard this from many leaders today. Oh, how the mighty have fallen with this cavalier approach to integrity. There is no difference—if you can cheat on your wife (the person closest to you), then you can also cheat in other areas in your life, including in your organization. There are *not* different *types* of integrity: integrity you use at the office or at church or in your personal life. It really is this simple. There is just one integrity. Integrity is integrity. Either you have it or you don't.

INTEGRITY IS INTEGRITY. EITHER YOU HAVE IT OR YOU DON'T.

THE PROCESS OF BEING INTEGRAL

I read an interesting book called *Overcoming the Dark Side of Leadership* by Gary L. McIntosh and Samuel D. Rima. In this book, the authors present a theory to show that the issues that compel people to become successful leaders are usually the same issues that precipitate their failure. The book goes on to help leaders understand, discover and redeem their dark sides. There is a dark side to each of us, and the sooner we understand and discover our dark sides, the sooner we can redeem them. We need to put precautions in place to prevent our dark sides from constantly rearing their ugly heads in our lives.

The process of being integral is just that—a process. I'm not sure we will ever get to that perfect state of being integral. Even if you think you've reached the perfect state, maintaining your integrity will be even harder than getting there. You may never be truly whole, but you must commit to working at it. That is the challenge with integrity—it's so powerful that the closer we get to it, the closer we get to see the world as God intended.

We can continually build on our journeys towards integrity. Here are two steps to help you:

1) Develop your integrity daily.

At the beginning of each day, take some time to learn more about yourself and how you can further develop your integrity. There are many good resources out there that you can use to help with your development. For me personally, I have a routine of trying to read a few of King Solomon's proverbs each morning and grasp at least one of his principles. However you choose to do this doesn't matter. The importance is to just do it.

2) Guard your integrity daily.

At the end of each day, reflect on your day and review areas in your life where you may have fallen short. It's important to recognize these areas of failure so that you become acutely aware of them, diminish them and prevent them from happening again. The process of guarding your integrity daily acts as a roadblock and constant marker to ensure you're moving forward, not backward, on your journey of integrity.

Integrity is a quality we cannot fake. There is no such thing as insincere integrity. If it is insincere, then it is not integrity. We need to ask ourselves, *Where am I with my integrity?* or *Do I have integrity?* These are critical questions. We cannot fake it.

INTEGRITY IS A QUALITY WE CANNOT FAKE.

CHAPTER 5

LEADERS CAN BE MADE

Leaders must be tough enough to fight, tender enough to cry, human enough to make mistakes, humble enough to admit them, strong enough to absorb the pain, and resilient enough to bounce back and keep on moving.
—Jesse Jackson

In this chapter, we'll be looking at the third letter in the acronym **PILOT—L** for **L**eaders.

In October 2014, Malala Yousafzai was announced as the co-recipient of the Nobel Peace Prize at the age of seventeen. She was the youngest person to receive this prize and the recognition was "for their struggle against the suppression of children and young people and for the right of all children to education." Her story is told at www.NobelPrize.org:

Malala Yousafzai was born in the Swat district of northwestern Pakistan, where her father was a school owner and was active in educational issues. After having blogged for the BBC since 2009 about her experiences during the Taliban's growing influence in the region, in 2012 the Taliban attempted to assassinate Malala Yousafzai on the bus home from school. She survived, but underwent several operations in the UK, where she lives today. In addition to her schooling, she continues her work for the right of girls to education."

While leaders come in all shapes, forms and sizes, there are certain key attributes that they possess that set them apart from others. Let's look deeper into some key questions around the concept of leadership and leaders and also explore the attributes fundamental for an aspiring leader:

- What is leadership?
- What do leaders do?
- Are leaders born or made?
- The DNA for future leaders
- Building blocks for everyday leadership

WHAT IS LEADERSHIP?

Let's start by exploring what leadership really is.

- "Leadership is influence—nothing more, nothing less." —Dr. John Maxwell
- "Being a great leader is all about having a genuine willingness and a true commitment to lead others to achieve a common vision and goals through positive influence. No leader can ever achieve anything great or long-lasting all alone. Teamwork goes hand in hand with leadership." —Dr. John Maxwell

- "Leadership is a function of knowing yourself, having a vision that is well communicated, building trust among colleagues, and taking effective action to realize your own leadership potential." —Warren Bennis, pioneer of the contemporary field of leadership studies

- "Leadership is the art of getting someone else to do something you want done because he wants to do it." —Dwight D. Eisenhower

I could go on highlighting the many definitions of leadership, but I'll stop there. I don't think I'm qualified or smart enough to add another profound leadership definition to the thousands that already exist. But I do want to map out a *functional approach to leadership.*

In our journey towards establishing LeaderGrow, we designed a specific DNA that I'm convinced is *integral* for leaders. Before we unpack this DNA, please allow me to at least attempt to add my simple definition of leadership. This is not to contradict my earlier statement. This definition is aligned to the specific organizational DNA that we'll be unpacking. My simple definition of leadership is: Leadership is a heart issue. It is about a leader's heart. Nothing more, nothing less.

LEADERSHIP IS A HEART ISSUE. IT IS ABOUT A LEADER'S HEART. NOTHING MORE, NOTHING LESS.

Leadership Is All about the Heart.

Growing up, I was intrigued by the biblical account of King David. He is one of the most important figures in Jewish history. Born in 907 BC, he reigned as king of Israel for forty years and died at the age of seventy in 837 BC. There is so much that can be said about this king. Some people like to focus on his warrior aspects, but, when his persona and accomplishments are considered as a whole, it's his spiritual greatness that shines the most.

David, son of Jesse, was a forgotten young shepherd boy before God's providence resulted in his being raised up as ruler of Israel. David became the most celebrated king the nation had ever had as it thrived under his leadership. However, David was far from perfect. In fact, he was a man of contrasts. At times he was single-mindedly devoted to God, yet at other times he failed miserably and committed some of the most serious sins recorded in the Old Testament. This is what drew me into researching him. Because of David's bloody, battle-scarred record, as well as his adulterous relationship with Bathsheba and the slaying of her husband, God denied His otherwise faithful servant the honor of building His temple. This must have been a big disappointment to David, yet God assured him that He would still make his name the greatest on earth. God established the throne of David forever, albeit through David's son, Solomon. Why would God do this for David when he was *not* a perfect king and leader?

The answer is simple. God chose David because of his heart. In 1 Samuel 16:7 (NIV), it says, "But the Lord said to Samuel, do not consider his appearance or his height . . . The LORD does not look at the things people look at. People look at the outward appearance, but the LORD looks at the heart." David was a man after God's own heart, and this was what God always looked at, even during the times when David was far from perfect. During those times of imperfection, David's broken heart and contrite spirit brought him the forgiveness of God. David was sincere with God. He opened up and honestly shared his thoughts, struggles and fears. David's first and foremost drive was to have a relationship with God. Throughout his life, David loved God deeply and passionately.

In our modern age, status, image and outward appearance play important roles in choosing our leaders. Educational background, physical attractiveness, social standing, knowledge, skills and experience, important as they are, are not the most important qualifications. As can been seen with David, the inner condition of the human heart is most important to God. Therefore, it's my view, that this is the most important qualification for preparing a leader to lead successfully. In David, God *saw* a caring heart, a servant heart, an honest heart, a faithful and loyal heart, a patient heart, a teachable heart and an obedient heart. David certainly had his faults, but it was his heart as a leader that God always focused on. It is this kind of heart that I believe is necessary to develop in every leader of tomorrow. Leadership is all about the heart—it's about having a heart for the people and a heart for the cause. What is the condition of your heart as a leader?

WHAT DO LEADERS DO?

The second question I want to explore is this: What do leaders actually do? Before we dive into their key attributes and characteristics,

I want to take a more theoretical look into what leaders do or what their duties are.

Kings and Priests

Back in 2009, when my vision was being established to raise "kings and priests," I began a journey of self-discovery to better understand this vision. During this period, I began to understand that a king and a priest were two types of leaders in medieval society. According to the *Oxford English Dictionary*, a king was "the male ruler of an independent state, especially one who inherits the position by right of birth." For example, Henry VIII was a king. A priest was "an ordained minister of the Catholic, Orthodox or Anglican church, authorized to perform certain rites and administer certain sacraments." Kings and priests performed certain key duties as leaders. Understanding these duties has helped me understand what is required from leaders, even though this may be construed as being theoretical or even impersonal in nature.

The duties of a king can be described under the categories of securing the property (physical land and its boundaries), securing the progeny (royal succession) and securing the divine presence (temple and religious rituals). In his article "Prophet, Priest, and King," posted at *Remnant Resource*, Doug Ponder stated, "Kings ruled over God's people as an extension of God's own rule ... [and] were also symbolic reminders of God's power and authority." The details of their oath varied from one land to another, but included the responsibility to keep the peace, administer justice and uphold the law. The duties of a priest were described under the headings of sacrifice, purification, divination and teaching the law. Ponder went on to say, "They were mediators between God and His people. They served the people on God's behalf and represented the people before God Himself."

Let's summarize the keywords and phrases describing the duties of kings and priests in medieval times:

- secure the property
- secure the progeny
- secure the divine presence
- keep the peace
- administer justice
- uphold the law
- sacrifice
- purification
- divination
- teaching

This is a significant list of duties that kings and priests needed to perform.

After researching and reviewing many theoretical approaches to the duties of leaders, two key themes recur:

1) A leader needs to have a good heart.

2) A leader needs to have a solid foundation.

ARE LEADERS BORN OR MADE?

Thirdly, I want to challenge the age-old controversial question: Are leaders born or made?

I've had many debates around this topic over the years. My initial instinct was that leaders were born with an inherent natural gift to lead and that there are certain inborn characteristics that predisposed people to be leaders and become leaders. I wasn't alone in my belief as during the early twentieth century trait theories, which were widely accepted, supported the notion that leaders are born. The basic premise of trait theories is that leaders became leaders because they possess physical, mental and social traits, which others do not. If you look at some of the great leaders of that time, like Alexander the Great, William Wallace and King Arthur, they certainly support trait theories. These great men did indeed possess unique qualities that were different from the average man.

Dr. Chand, in his book *What's Shaking Your Ladder?* asserts that "leaders are made the way that bread is made."

Leadership development is an intentional activity. Raisin bread doesn't appear by itself, even if we leave the ingredients on the kitchen counter overnight. Someone must consciously take ingredients and knead them together, put the mixture under the right amount of heat and allow it to rise, only to punch it down and start over again until the dough is the perfect consistency. Only then will it rise above the pan and taste delicious. Helping a leader rise takes this same kind of intentional activity.

As LeaderGrow has become established, my opinion of leaders being born has started to shift. This is purely based on the changes we've seen in the many young leaders that have gone through our LeaderGrow programs. During the past few years, we've had all kinds of "ordinary" people register. They've ranged in ages, races and religious backgrounds. They've differed from sacred to secular fields, from government institutions to large corporations and from experienced leaders to people that have never led in their lives. Seeing first-hand how their lives and leadership abilities got better and better, when provided with the intentional leadership development we were providing, has been inspirational. As I'm writing this, images of the many young leaders whose lives have been impacted by our programs flood my mind. For me, there is no greater feeling in the world than having people stop you at the airport or write you an email or send you a text message expressing their heartfelt thanks for the role you've played in their leadership development and in their lives.

Personally, I never saw myself as a born leader, and I think that's why I was driven to study the principles of leadership. I always aspired to be a good leader, but I was never the obvious choice because I didn't fit the model type for a leader. Even my introverted personality seemed to count against me. So you can say that intentional leadership development also helped me improve my leadership skills. My experiences have taught me that (1) everyone plays a leader role in some way or the other in life and (2) with intentional leadership development EVERYONE can improve his or her leadership ability—leaders can be made. Not everyone is going to be able to lead in the limelight of today's society and be recognized as such, like the CEO of Coca-Cola or the captain of the Springbok rugby team, but everyone does lead.

For example, my wife, Kirbashnee, leads my household (whether I like it or not), and she is the glue that holds our family together. I admire how she is positively leading my two daughters to become integral leaders. She is sometimes never noticed, but one day I assured her that she would be recognized as the central, most influential figure in the lives of both my daughters. Arianna is already leading many groups in her school, and Alessandra leads her divas around the playground each day. Their birthday parties are always over-attended, and it's not because of the elaborate parties that Kirbashnee throws, which always test my bank account. No, it is because my two girls are leading their peer groups and therefore have many followers. And it is our job to make sure that we continue intentionally developing them into integral leaders of tomorrow.

When we started LeaderGrow, we wanted to make it accessible to all people, and not just to a selection of privileged people that have the financial or large corporate resources to continue their leadership development. We believed that if we could positively develop a leader's heart, then it would positively impact a family, a community, a city and a nation. I now believe that you can develop people into integral leaders, moving them from ordinary to exceptional, and take what is in their hearts to equip them for self-leadership and the leadership of others. I stumbled into my development as a leader. Many others may not be that fortunate, so it's necessary to create a platform that is inclusive and intentional for people to become integral leaders of tomorrow.

Now I'm ready to admit that leaders can be made; the ingredients are there. That's where you and I come in. Imagine what people can accomplish if we invest the necessary time to develop them into tomorrow's leaders?

THE DNA FOR FUTURE LEADERS

Again, I believe that leadership is a heart issue, so my focus has always been on developing a leader's heart. I've advocated a leadership style that is principles-led and values-based, whereby a leader's character is at the center, and relationships are key (transactions are secondary). In light of this, I believe that a specific DNA is necessary for future leaders if they are to make a lasting and positive impact in the world. The foundation of this DNA is the heart. As a leader's heart gets developed, the other DNA characteristics also get shaped and molded. Other DNA characteristics are necessary for successful leadership in future too.

Love

Leaders need to love more. One of the basic human needs is love. We all desire to be loved, so leaders need to love the people they lead. This isn't the superficial love prevalent among many leaders today. I'm talking about love and compassion for their people that *deeply* moves leaders' hearts to want to help make their people's lives better.

Mateo Sol, guest writer for *Wake Up World*, described "Eight Different Types of Love According to the Ancient Greeks" in his January 25, 2019, article. However, it is *agape* or selfless love that the Greeks considered "the highest and most radical" type. "This type of love is not the sentimental outpouring that often passes as love in our society. It has nothing to do with the condition-based type of love that our sex-obsessed culture tries to pass as love."

Agape love is what some people call spiritual love. It's an unconditional love that's bigger than ourselves; a boundless compassion and an infinite empathy. Sol goes on to say that *agape* is "the purest form of love that is free from desires and expectations and loves regardless of the flaws and shortcomings of others. Agape is the love that accepts, forgives and believes for our greater good." This is the love that should be in the DNA for any successful leader. It's that love that permeates all spheres of life and people for the greater good of mankind. It's the purest form of love in a leader's heart.

Serve

Let me break this to you gently. Leaders need to serve. A leader's job is not to be served, but to serve others. Leaders don't show off their authority over others. Instead, they serve and do whatever is best for their people—their team, organization, small group or followers. They don't look out for what's best for them. How often have we gotten this concept wrong? Servant leadership is a leadership style that many believe shows the weakness and vulnerability of a leader, but in reality, it's the truest measure of leadership ability.

For me, as a Christian, the greatest example of a servant leader is Jesus Christ. The fundamental belief of Christians is that Jesus Christ was God incarnate (divine), yet He came to serve. Jesus Christ Himself is recorded in the New Testament saying, "Your attitude must be like my own, for I, the Messiah, did not come to be served, but to serve, and to give my life as a ransom for many" (Matthew 20:28, TLB). Throughout the Bible, there are numerous examples of Jesus Christ serving. He served His disciples by washing their feet, He served the multitudes by taking care of all their needs and He served His Father by giving up His own life for the world.

For many, serving others is not a natural part of their personalities. Most of the time, we'd like people to serve us. However, Robert Greenleaf believes, according to his 1970 essay "The Servant as Leader," this:

If a better society is to be built, one that is more just and more loving, one that provides greater creative opportunity for its people, then the most open course is to raise both the capacity to serve and the very performance as servant of existing major institutions by new regenerative forces operating within them.

Leaders must become like servants to their people and make sure they put the needs of the people they lead before their own.

Care

Leaders need to care, and care deeply. Great leaders care more about those they lead than themselves. Because they care, they lead with courage to do what is right rather than what is easiest. There is a golden rule that every leader should learn: "Do unto others as you want done unto you."

I'm sure you've also heard this popular phrase: "People won't care how much you know until they know how much you care." Leaders who get to know their people can tailor efforts to personalize the experience of care to the individual.

"PEOPLE WON'T CARE HOW MUCH YOU KNOW UNTIL THEY KNOW HOW MUCH YOU CARE."

A few years back, I was asked to take on a sales and marketing role. I inherited a very diverse team, and I didn't know anyone well. It was also a substantially large team, but I took the risk of breaking down all reporting structures and made everyone report directly to me for the first year. I deliberately did this as I wanted to spend the first year getting to know each person personally and, more importantly, developing personal care for them. While it was an extremely tough year managing each person in the team individually, the benefit was that I developed a team that knew I genuinely cared for them as unique individuals and not just as employees.

In the February 28, 2017, article "Great Leaders Show Genuine Care for Their Teams," in *Harvard Business Review*, Bruce Jones described this: "Employees who feel personally and consistently cared for are more likely to pay individual attention to not only their customers and colleagues." I'd venture to say this applies to their work too. This was evident in my team. We genuinely cared about each other and the work we did. Richard Branson once said, "The way you treat your employees is the way they will treat your customers." Leaders that truly care demonstrate three characteristics: patience, loyalty and kindness. That is what needs to be instilled in leaders—a heart of genuine care.

Inspire

Leaders need to inspire and provide hope. Vince Lombardi said, "*Leadership* is based on a spiritual quality; the power to *inspire*, the power to *inspire* others to follow."

The 1995 Rugby World Cup in South Africa was a defining moment in the history of our democracy. Nelson Mandela said,

Sport has the power to change the world. It has the power to inspire. It has the power to unite people in a way that little else

does. It speaks to youth in a language they understand. Sport can create hope where once there was only despair. It is more powerful than government in breaking down racial barriers.

In 1992, South Africa had been awarded the opportunity to host the Rugby World Cup. Madiba allowed the competition to proceed even though rugby was regarded as a white sport. The national team, the Springboks, had only one non-white player, and South African black people largely refused to support the team. For many, the green Springbok jersey was a symbol of apartheid. But Madiba wanted the nation to support the Springboks. He bravely wore the Springbok jersey of the team captain, a white Afrikaner, before a crowd of sixty-five thousand almost completely white people. Miraculously, the crowd, silent at first, began chanting, "Nelson! Nelson! Nelson!"

This act inspired the country, including the Springbok team that didn't have much of a chance of beating the mighty New Zealand All Blacks team in the final. The Springboks went on to win the game and South Africans, both black and white, were seen hugging each other all over the country as they celebrated the victory. This was the same country where hatred existed between blacks and whites. Madiba's inspired leadership created a new, hope-filled future for his nation. Leaders need to inspire and create hope for their people.

Inspirational leaders, not fast-talking con men, are what the world is crying out for. I recently read an article by Mental Toughness Partners titled "7 Ingredients for Inspirational Leadership." In this article, the author points out the following:

Passion, purpose, listening and meaning help make a leader inspirational. Exhibiting these qualities and characteristics is a

*must if you wish to inspire the best work from your employees.
An inspirational leader does not just tell employees that he or
she is deeply committed to their customer's experience. The
leader must demonstrate this commitment and passion in every
meeting, presentation, and in how the leader handles and tells
employees to handle customer woes. The leader's behavior must
inspire employees to act in the same way.*

Furthermore, according to an article by Eric Garton on "How to
Be an Inspiring Leader" published in the April 25, 2017 issue of the
Harvard Business Review, research showed that anyone can be an
inspiring leader. Once again, leaders are made, not born.

Hope

Leaders need to provide hope for their people. Joyce Meyer once
stated, "Hope is favorable and confident expectation; it's an expectant
attitude that something good is going to happen and things will work
out, no matter what situation we're facing." It's a positive attitude
and the happy anticipation that something good is going to happen.
Many have debated that selling hope is not a strategy. In her *Harvard
Business Review* blog article titled, "Hope Is a Strategy (Well, Sort
Of)," Deborah Mills-Scofield clearly articulates:

*Hope is a critical part of achieving a strategy when based on
what is possible; perhaps not highly probable, but possible. Hope
is the belief that something is possible and probable, and the recognition that the degree of each is not necessarily equal. When
hope is based on real-world experience, knowledge and tangible*

and intangible data, it results in trust, which is necessary to implementing any strategy.

Writer Glenn Llopis suggests "5 Ways Leaders Keep Hope Alive in Difficult Times":

- Hope renews faith.
- Hope builds self-confidence.
- Hope promotes empowerment and clarity.
- Hope helps increase productivity and underscores a positive work ethic.
- Hope instills family pride and togetherness.

Hope is a powerful human emotion, and leaders who are able to stir up and provide hope to their people, as part of their DNA, can use this attribute to do great things together.

Integrity

Leaders have no option but to lead with the highest degree of integrity. They have to be integral. In the previous chapter, we learned that leaders need to be incorruptible, sound, whole and complete. They need to be honest, reliable and consistent. Most importantly, leaders need to do the right thing when no one is watching. Leaders don't cheat, steal or manipulate people or systems to reach their goals. I believe that if you have integrity as a leader, you have everything. Your people know that you will lead soundly because you're assured of who you are. Integrity means you are true to your word. People can trust you because you do what you say.

LEADERS HAVE NO OPTION BUT TO LEAD WITH THE HIGHEST DEGREE OF INTEGRITY.

Humility

Leaders need to be humble. They lead from the front with humility and they lead from behind in support. They lead in a participative way. Leaders assess themselves appropriately. They understand, and act out of, their strengths and weaknesses. They recognize that they are no more important than any other person. However, humility in a leader does not mean weakness or meekness in their ability to lead. The best leaders are humble leaders. To be great, you have to be humble.

There are the five golden rules to humility:

1) Admit your mistakes.

2) Give credit but share blame.

3) Ask for constructive feedback.

4) Lead by actions not words.

5) Respect everyone.

Develop Other Leaders

Leaders develop other leaders. They act as role models. It is called transformational leadership. Leaders must leave people in a better condition than they were when they began leading them. Leaders don't drain their followers, take from them or use them for their own agendas. If you want to find a great leader, look for followers who are growing in joy, skill, capacity and output month after month.

Admit Mistakes

Leaders will make mistakes. However, leaders are quick to admit their mistakes and correct them with the right heart. Leaders are not responsible for always being right. As all great leaders will tell you, they've made many mistakes along the way; this is how they have learned. They learned more from their mistakes than when things were going well. That is the reality of life—we will learn more from our mistakes.

Successful leaders are transparent enough with themselves and others to admit their wrongdoings. There are several reasons why it's beneficial for leaders to do this: It shows humility. It earns respect. It shows one's human side and vulnerability. It encourages one's team to perform optimally and creatively without fear of making mistakes. And, it builds trust within the team and teamwork.

I've made many BIG mistakes in my corporate career. I can recall a recent incident where one of these mistakes was painful. It's much easier to look back on it now and review the lessons, but at that time it was one of the most unpleasant and hurtful experiences of my life. I could've just not admitted my mistake and tried to fix it, but I found the courage to first admit my mistake and then still try to fix it.

It's my experience, that when leaders make mistakes they have everything to gain by admitting them. When they don't, they have plenty to lose. Dale E. Turner once said, "It is the highest form of self-respect to admit our errors and mistakes and make amends for them. To make a mistake is only an error in judgement, but to adhere to it when it is discovered shows infirmity of character."

"A TRUE LEADER IS ONE WHO IS HUMBLE ENOUGH TO ADMIT THEIR MISTAKES." — JOHN MAXWELL

Gallup, a management consulting company, used its ability to research and analyze data to produce a book called *Strengths-Based Leadership* that is a must-read for any leader of a team or organization. Its research identified the four needs of followers: trust (honesty, respect and integrity); compassion (caring, friendship, happiness and love); stability (security, strength, support and peace) and hope (direction, faith and guidance).

I've also carefully studied great leaders that I've had the privilege to work with, and I've specifically tried to capture the key qualities that make them great. While my research is not on the scale of Gallup, it has led me to conclude that the above attributes and characteristics—loving, caring, serving, inspiring, hope, integrity, humility, developing other leaders and admitting mistakes—are certainly core to the DNA of any aspiring future leader. And it is this DNA that I wish to instill in future leaders. As you continue to grow as a leader, I encourage you to aspire to this DNA. You will be in the company of many others.

I hope you're gaining a better understanding of what leadership is and what it takes to be a leader. In addition, I trust that you agree with me now that leaders can be made, which is exciting for those of us that aren't seen as natural-born leaders. Leaders can be made like bread is made, but this process of making a leader is not an easy one!

CHAPTER 6

BUILDING BLOCKS FOR FUTURE LEADERS

n this chapter, we'll continue with the third letter in the acronym **PILOT**—**L** for **L**eaders.

So far, I've provided you with insights into several key building blocks that are required by future leaders to make their journeys successful. In the previous chapters, we covered *focus, vision casting* and *integrity*. Let's continue with four more that will help you with everyday leadership. They are:

1) Communication
2) Decision-making
3) Managing conflict
4) Strengths-based leadership

They are covered extensively in our **PILOT** program, but I've tried to summarize them in a manner which will still provide you with the key insights and lessons to equip and empower you along your leadership journey.

COMMUNICATION

I often use a practical example to demonstrate how communication is one of the biggest obstacles leaders face in organizations today. Try this: Select two teams of around eight people and line them up next to each other. Give the first person in each group a piece of paper with a little message and then ask them to relay the message down the telephone line. I often use: "If you notice this notice, you will notice that this notice is no longer a notice anymore." It's hilarious hearing the difference between the original messages given and the final messages reproduced by the last person in both groups. Herein lies the problem with all communication according to George Bernard Shaw: "The single biggest problem in communication is the illusion that it has taken place."

Concrete and Abstract Thinkers

LEADERS WHO ARE ABSTRACT THINKERS NEED TO BECOME CONCRETE COMMUNICATORS.

People are either concrete or abstract thinkers, and their communication style will follow their way of thinking. Leaders are generally abstract thinkers. They talk about their great visions and plans for their organizations. On the flip side, most of the people they lead are concrete thinkers whose brains are wired to think concretely. In other words, they want specifics and details for them to better understand what the leader is saying. The difference in communication styles is where the confusion starts in most organizations.

For example, a leader of an organization says, "We want to maintain sustainable and profitable growth through the next five years." It's a great vision, but it's also an abstract concept. The more concrete thinkers are thinking, *How do we do this in an already tough market? Do we need more customers? Are we going to cut costs? Do we scale down on some of our operations? Do we reduce complexity? Do we sell non-core assets?* They are also thinking, *What is the strategy and plan? When does this happen? Who does what? How will this now impact me?*

I recently made this mistake when I communicated to our local team that we'd be aligning our group's strategy. It wasn't long until I had a queue of people outside my office asking me what it meant for our non-core local businesses that are different from the group. I was asked, "Will there be retrenchments coming? Will the group be sending people to drive this alignment? How will this impact our current customer base?" This was because concrete thinkers take abstract statements and start asking specific questions. They even make their own assumptions of these abstract statements. When concrete thinkers don't have enough information, they take what they hear and fill in their own details.

This is a challenge for leaders as this is how we miscommunicate with our people. We don't consider how the concrete thinkers will receive our abstract messages. It gets even tougher because once these concrete thinkers have something in their minds regarding your abstract statements, it becomes difficult to get these thoughts out. You would need to spend much more time changing their minds, and we all know how tough it is to change people's mindsets. As leaders, we can be both concrete and abstract thinkers, but our employees may only be concrete thinkers. Therefore, leaders who are abstract thinkers need to become concrete communicators.

Communication Is Listening

Listening is pivotal to communication. Some of the greatest communicators were also the greatest listeners. God has given us two ears and one mouth for a reason. Communication should involve less talking and more listening. There is a distinct difference between hearing and listening. The American College of Healthcare and Technology describes it thus:

> *Hearing is simply the act of perceiving sound by the ear. If you are not hearing-impaired, hearing simply happens. Listening, however, is something you consciously choose to do. Listening requires concentration so that your brain processes meaning from words and sentences."*

Someone rightly said, "Hearing is through the ears, but listening is through the mind." The two activities of hearing and listening involve the use of ears, but they are different. Listening is difficult because it requires concentration and attention, and the human mind is easily distracted.

For great communication, you need to be more than just a good listener. You need to be an *active listener*. Active listening takes your skills to the next level. Active listening is the key element that makes the communication process effective. It's as its name suggests—actively listening—and it requires the involvement of all of your senses. A leader must fully focus and feel what's being said, rather than just listening to the words of the person. Active listening is a difficult skill to master, but one that needs to be learned and developed for successful leadership.

There are certain techniques you can use to ensure that you're actively listening:

- *Verbal and non-verbal messages*: These include maintaining eye contact, nodding your head and using phrases like "okay," "yes" or "aha."
- *Paraphrasing*: Every few minutes, try to paraphrase what the person has just said to make sure you have both understood exactly what has been communicated. Then ask if your understanding is correct or anything needs to be clarified before continuing.
- *Summarize and recap*: At the end of the conversation, try to summarize and recap what has just been communicated. Ask again for confirmation and further clarification before you communicate your thoughts.

Bad Communication Habits

There are certain common and courteous communication habits that you have to master in the corporate world in order to be successful. There are also bad communication habits that you need to avoid:

■ Not responding to telephone calls or emails

It baffles me that people can have such wonderful voicemail invitations, but never return calls. These people are lying that they will get back to you. Always return phone calls—no matter how minute or immaterial the messages may be!

In the same vein, always respond to emails. If you think the email is going to take some time to draft, go back to the sender and at least acknowledge the email. Simply explain that you'll get back to them within a certain time period. Furthermore, when writing emails, it doesn't take a lot of effort to address your salutations appropriately and professionally. A simple "Dear Mr. X" or "Kind regards" is important for leaders to set the right example of professionalism, care and respect.

■ Communicating only when you need something

I'm guilty of this one, and the biggest victim is my wife. Kirbashnee tries so hard to communicate with me, but I'm often so preoccupied with "things" that I'm *hearing* her but not *listening* to her. However, when I need something from her (which is often), I tend to pull out the charm. People see right through this bad habit when leaders only talk to people when they need something, even if they ask nicely for it. It says to the person, "You're not important; this is just a master and slave relationship."

■ Not following up

There's a huge difference between not following up and micromanaging. One of the biggest failures of executives in the twenty-first century is poor execution. It is key for any leader to manage risks and ensure things are getting done. By not following up (asking who does what, by when), leaders face the risk of things not getting done or not getting done on time. Larry Bossidy and Ram Charan wrote a book with Charles Burck titled *Execution: The Discipline of Getting Things Done*. In it, they propose that the biggest gap in leadership right now is the gap between what is said and what is done. In other words, a lack of follow-through. We need to hold people accountable. We can do this by ending our meetings, emails and conversations with a few key questions:

What is the next step?

When will it be completed?

By whom?

■ Lack of basic courtesy

Leaders need to watch their Ps and Qs. I'm sometimes stunned at a leader's lack of basic courtesy both in the office and out. A simple "please" or "thank you" isn't difficult, yet it goes a long way to show people respect. Think how the atmosphere around the office could change if everybody used basic courtesy?

■ Negativity

Negative people will always be around us. But something worse than a negative person is a negative leader. The most important thing a leader can do for his or her people is to keep them motivated even though the storms are coming. I'm asking you not to be unrealistic, but to maintain hope, keep a positive attitude and open the team up to some blue-sky thinking.

During one of my tenures, I was responsible for a stable business that had been around for decades, but this business was not going to shoot the lights out with tremendous growth. Being the new kid on the block, I wanted to freshen up the team and get some positive juices flowing, even with some of the "older" members of the executive team. However, it didn't take me long to figure out that these "older" guys had seen it all, and every new idea was always shot down with, "We can't do that; it's not possible." So I decided to play a game. During each meeting, we introduced a special jar and if anyone said something that couldn't be done that person would have to put a predetermined amount of money into the jar. We were to use this money at the end of the year, however we wished. By month three, we could solve the world's problems with our positive mindset.

A MODEL FOR COMMUNICATION

There are many models for communication. However, I want to introduce a simple communication model that we adopt in our **PILOT** program which has helped me and may also be useful to you. The communication model is as follows:

1) *Listening*—Actively listen to what the person is saying or trying to say. Often the first question isn't the real question. The second question is the one people really want answered. Observe a person's body language.

2) *Asking questions*—Asking questions shows the person that you are actually listening and that you care. It also makes sure that you're accurately following the conversation and getting to the real question or issue that the person is communicating.

3) *Understanding*—The first rule we can learn from Steven Covey's *Seven Habits of Highly Effective People* is "seek first to understand." By understanding, I'm referring to making sure

you've sought to fully comprehend the issues being communicated. There are no ambiguities.

4) *Answering*—If you follow the above process, then you will be in a position to answer effectively.

The ability to communicate effectively is a key building block to ensure leadership success. Make sure your communication isn't an illusion.

DECISION-MAKING

Leaders are required to make decisions every day. Sometimes, many decisions in a day. It goes with the territory of being a leader. I get faced with this challenge on a daily basis. It's not uncommon for there to be a line of people waiting outside my office, and it's usually not for a social visit. They always want a decision from me. It occurred to me that I've been trained in many aspects of business, but no one ever trained me on how to make decisions. The decisions we make are largely dependent on the types of leaders we are.

Situational Versus Principled Decision-Makers

Leaders can be categorized into two types of decision makers. They are either situational decision makers or principled decision makers. The type of decision maker you are will impact the decisions you make, and the decisions you make will communicate who you are as a leader.

Situational decision makers make decisions based on the here and now. They make decisions to ensure they avoid potential crises. Situational decision makers rarely consider the future consequences of their decisions. People who work for situational decision makers are often insecure as they never know what type of decision their leaders will make. Situational decision makers are inconsistent in their decision-making.

Principled decision makers will make a decision based on what is right, not on what is easiest. People love working with principled decision makers because they feel secure; they know that decisions will be consistent. In fact, people that work for principled decision makers most likely already know the decision their leader will make. Principled decision makers take into account the future consequences of their decisions. I always teach leaders in our organization to ask the following question when making a decision, "What is the right thing to do?" As leaders, we should strive to, "Do what is right. Always." Whenever I'm making a decision, after assessing all the information, I always ask myself that question before I make the decision. After I've made the decision, I ask myself again, "Was this the right thing to do?" By doing this, I'm testing that a principled decision, no matter how difficult the decision was, has been made.

What type of decision maker are you?

You're probably thinking, *Easy for you to say, but I'm not sure you understand the pressures I face to produce results.* Maybe not, but I think I've been in enough of these positions in my life to understand the pressures that exist. They can't be an excuse to make unprincipled decisions.

Earlier I mentioned that we're facing some big corporate scandals in South Africa. One of these centered on a company called Steinhoff International. The ex-CEO resigned and admitted that he made some big mistakes that were classified as "accounting irregularities."

While we applauded this ex-CEO for admitting his mistakes, the question that should have been asked was, "For how long had he and his executives been making situational decisions?" The company has lost around eighty-five percent of its share value since the scandal broke. It was one of the top ten companies by market capitalization listed on the Johannesburg Stock Exchange (JSE), but risked falling out of the JSE top 100 as its market capital plummeted to around US$1.5 billion from about US$15.5 billion as of December 2017. What is interesting is that in early December 2017, Steinhoff said that its 2017 audited financial statements would be delayed, and then further went on to say that it would need to restate its 2016 and 2015 financial statements. Again, "For how long had he and his executives been making situational decisions?" In short, these decisions stood to cripple this massive international company with close to twelve thousand stores in thirty countries that employ over 130,000 people.

During the COVID-19 pandemic, global leaders were called on to make vital decisions. Many of these leaders made situational decisions and many made principled ones. We'll need to wait on history to see which decision makers got this right, but I can hazard a guess which ones I'll put my money on.

A MODEL FOR DECISION-MAKING

Here is a simple decision-making model that we include in our **PILOT** programs:

1) Gather data
2) Select relevant information

3) Combine with pre-existing knowledge

4) Make decision

The most common steps include gathering data, sorting out the information that is relevant to the decision, combining it with our knowledge and then ultimately making a decision. As you get more familiar with this model, most of these steps will happen unconsciously. Let's use a practical application of this decision-making process by using an example—which I have slighted adapted—found in Dr. Chand's book *What's Shaking your Ladder?*

Let's say that Natalie lives in the city of Vienna, Austria, and needs to travel by car to Prague, Czech Republic, for her grandma's ninetieth birthday party. Doesn't seem like much of a decision, does it? Natalie loves her cooking, and nothing is better than spending Sunday dinner at Grandma's house since she always makes a feast. But to get to her house while the mashed potatoes are still hot, Natalie has to make many decisions. Here's one: How will she get to Grandmother's house?

Step 1: Data Collection

During this step, we collect all of the data that we need or could possibly need. For Natalie, that data might include the answers to these questions:

- What time does dinner start?
- How early does she need to get there to get a seat at the adult table?
- What time does the Sunday church service start and end at her church?

- Does she need to go home first, or can she leave directly after church?
- How long does it take to get to Grandma's?
- Will she be hungry when she gets there?
- Which highway does she need to take?
- Which is the fastest route? Safest route?

Once Natalie has gathered all the pieces of data, she selects the important ones and then summarizes and categorizes them. Finally, she analyses them and makes calculations based on the data.

Step 2: Select Relevant Information

At this point, Natalie has to select which pieces of data are relevant to her decision. Whether or not she'll be hungry and the topic of the minister's sermon on Sunday won't affect her travel plans, so she can safely eliminate those pieces. By comparing and connecting the other bits of data, she can get information that's actually useful. Here are some pieces that will be meaningful for the decision she is about to make:

- She plans to attend the church service at her church.
- It ends at 11:00 am.
- Grandma wants her at her place by 5:00 pm.
- There are several ways to get there. If she decides to go via Route 38 and highway D1/E65, it will take approximately three hours and thirty minutes.
- Currently there is construction on Route 38, and the traffic could delay her up to one hour. If she takes highway E49 it will take her close to four hours, but there isn't any construction.

Step 3: Combine with Pre-Existing Knowledge

Now that Natalie has the relevant information, she can combine it with her pre-existing knowledge, such as the fact that if she is late for dinner not only will Grandma be mad, but her cousins will finish off Grandma's famous pecan pie.

Step 4: Make Decision

At this point, Natalie decides that she'll take highway E49 because, while it may not get her there earlier, it will ensure that she is at Grandma's house on time. And the consequences of being late (and missing Grandma's pecan pie) are too great. Decision made.

We follow these steps each time we make a decision, but with most decisions, we do it so fast that we aren't conscious of it. Regardless of the content, these steps are involved. There will be times when your people will make bad decisions. Instead of coming down hard on them, use this as an opportunity to communicate. Review the decision making model with them to try to understand the process they followed in making their decision. Identifying our blind spots in decision-making will help to mitigate future mistakes.

FOUR QUESTIONS TO ASK BEFORE ACTING

Sometimes, the decisions we're facing aren't as simple as getting to Grandma's birthday party but are much more complex and complicated. This is especially true when presented with a decision that could change an organization and impact its people. In these cases, we need to ask four additional questions, and it is important that we ask them *in this order* before acting on a decision.

1) Is it in line with our vision, mission and core values?

No matter how great an idea or opportunity, if it isn't in line with the vision, we must say no to it.

2) Do we have the organizational and human capacity to do this? Do we have the heart for this?

Maybe the program is so large that it would consume the entire team. Maybe we don't have the right people on the team to make this happen. Or maybe we don't want to do it at this time.

3) Who will get the credit, and who will benefit?

Answering this question will help us to understand the true impact this decision will have. For example, "How will this decision serve my organization?" Insecure leaders want to soak up the credit for any success, but they quickly point fingers when things go wrong. Strong, gifted leaders give plenty of credit to everyone who contributed to the success of any venture. Those who benefit may be the team, the organization, the customers or the community. Having the credit and benefit in mind clarifies direction and heightens motivation.

4) How much will it cost?

Understand this question, and then consider it carefully. It's not, "Can we afford it?" Most organizations don't have money sitting around waiting to be used. The answer is usually no. But the answer to, "How much will it cost?" is different. The cost includes not only money, but people, resources and the time and energy pulled from other projects and programs.

A program that won't make it past the question, "Can we afford it?" might get a different response after asking these four questions. If the vision is big enough, if the people have a heart for doing it and if the right benefits are achieved, then the money will come. Answering these specific questions in this order helps us understand the true opportunity before us. We'll then be making a principled decision based on a larger organizational context, not on a situation.

Heart, Head, Hands

Finally, in the overall decision-making process, do not leave out your heart when making a decision. How often have we heard the phrase, "Take the emotions out of the decision"? I wonder what would happen if we used this same logic when selecting a spouse or buying our dream car or house? When we make life decisions, we follow the logic of feel, think, do. After all, we're human beings and that means we have feelings and emotions. We can't take our feelings or emotions out of decisions; otherwise, we'd simply be robots doing a job.

LET'S NOT FORGET OUR HEARTS DURING OUR DECISION-MAKING PROCESS.

When I made the life decision to marry my wife, the first thing that moved me towards this, apart from her good looks, was something that happened inside my heart. I started having these "funny" feelings inside of me every time I saw her and thought of her. This led me to start thinking that maybe she was the one. I started thinking about what my life would like look with her in it, what it would be like having kids with her and whether I could support her and a family. Finally, I took the final step of asking her to marry me, and the rest is history, twenty years later.

We need to use this process to make our leadership decisions. The sequence is "feel, think, do" or "heart, head, hands."

- Heart is the **WHY**—feelings, passion and beliefs
- Head is the **WHAT**—knowledge and understanding
- Hands is the **HOW**—the activity

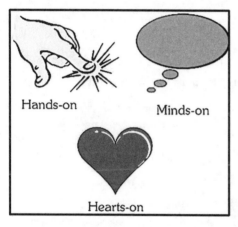

Hands-on

Minds-on

Hearts-on

In Decision Making

1. How do we make life decisions?
   —Feel, Think, Do
2. How are we making decisions currently?
   —Number of daily decisions
3. What is the sequence of decision making?
   —Heart, Head, Hands
   OR
   —Feel, Think, Do

We tend to make decisions with our heads and hands and leave out our hearts, but this is the wrong way. Let's not forget our hearts during our decision-making processes.

MANAGING CONFLICT

We all have conflict—at home, at the office and with our best friends. No matter how hard we try, we can never escape or avoid conflict. Living in South Africa, there is a good chance that you'll encounter many conflict situations, even just driving to the office each day. The only person that doesn't have conflict is a dead person. As long as you're alive and well, you're going to have conflict. So we'd better be in a position to manage and deal with conflict situations. We cover an intensive module on managing conflict in our **PILOT** program, and I could write another book just on managing conflict alone. However, for now, I'm going to provide just a few salient lessons that'll help you manage conflict as a leader.

The Definition of Conflict

Conflict can simply be defined as the difference between expectation and reality. Let's review the diagrams below to better understand.

Expectation:
All first-time flyers expect what they see in the movies—the grandeur of a flat bed with beautiful air hostesses waiting on them.

Reality:
The reality is that we're often stuck behind some big guy who thinks his seat is also a flat bed.

CONFLICT = the difference between EXPECTATION and REALITY

Another example is closer to home for us men. Assume that I decide to go on a night out with the boys. I say to Kirbashnee that I'm going out, but I'll be back home by 11 p.m. I actually get home at 4 a.m. Do you think this will give rise to a conflict?

Let's review:

- Kirbashnee had an expectation that I would be home by 11 p.m.
- The reality was that I got home at 4 a.m.

We can safely say that this is a classic conflict situation. In my home, I can taste a conflict situation (literally) as my dinners are usually a lot spicier than I'm used to. I can almost picture my wife over the stove, angrily adding tablespoons of chili powder, hoping that that will teach me a good lesson. Well, darling, if you're reading this—that is not the way to manage conflict situations.

Importance and Benefits of Conflict

As leaders, we need to understand that conflict is neither good nor bad. It simply is. There's no such thing as a conflict-free zone. As long as you're a living and active human being, there'll always be conflict.

THE DECISION-MAKING PROCESS IS MORE IMPORTANT THAN THE DECISION ITSELF.

There are actually certain benefits to conflict. Some of these include:

- Issues are now fully explored.
- Leaders look deeper into decisions to ensure they have all the information.

■ People are committed to the final decision because they are now involved.

Resolve conflict must involve dialogue between the opposing parties, as avoidance is not a tactic. We need to also take cognizance that the decision making-process is more important than the decision itself. Most leaders don't like conflict or don't like managing conflict. For any leader to be successful, he or she needs to be skilled in managing conflict. For leaders, there will always be conflict, unless their organizations are dead. Our job as leaders is to minimize the blood on the floor.

Managing Conflict Better

There are a few things leaders need to develop when managing conflict situations.

First, your health determines your response to conflict. You can only manage a conflict situation if you're healthy inside. I'm not talking about being physically healthy. I'm referring to being "heart healthy." If your heart is healthy, that is if your heart is objective, forgiving and unhurt, then you'll be in a position to manage the conflict better. The goal of conflict isn't to end it in agreement or disagreement. The goal is ongoing health. We need to honestly assess our own health first. If we're unhealthy then we should avoid trying to resolve conflict at that point, as it will make the conflict situation worse.

Let's say that you have a deep cut on your forearm. If you're not in good physical health, that cut can turn septic, become a bigger issue and may even require some sort of surgery to get well again. However, if you're a healthy person, that deep cut will scab and heal on its own with no further damage. We can only help others be healthy if we are healthy. Healthy people can go through conflict and heal from it.

Secondly, when managing conflict always focus on the WHAT—not the WHO. Focus on the issue (the WHAT) and not on the person (the WHO). The moment you move the discussion from the WHAT to the WHO, the conflict situation will escalate further. There may be situations where the WHO is the problem. Dr. John Maxwell refers to these people as "conflict carriers," and we need to deal with conflict carriers, but this is secondary and not important for now.

In summary, leaders will never escape managing conflict. We need to accept the fact that conflict simply is. It is natural. It happens. And leaders need to figure how to manage it.

STRENGTHS-BASED LEADERSHIP

The last building block in this chapter is the philosophy of strengths-based leadership. I'm sure many of you have been through annual performance reviews where your weaknesses are identified and then logged into a development plan. Over the next few years, you're then encouraged to work on these weaknesses to improve them through on-the-job coaching, internal and external training programs, self-awareness programs and so on. While I fully support a process for understanding one's weaknesses and improving on them, I'd prefer to use the philosophy of strengths-based leadership where an individual is required to focus and work harder on his or her strengths than weaknesses.

Let me use a sporting analogy to demonstrate. In the game of cricket, we have batsmen and bowlers. A batsman's strength is that he can bat, and a bowler's strength is that he can bowl. Imagine if the team gets to practice on the afternoon before a big match, and the coach decides to get the batsmen to spend the entire session practicing their bowling and the bowlers to spend the entire session practicing their batting. I do agree that there'll be times in a cricket game when a bowler has to come in at a crucial stage to bat, so bowlers should spend some time working on their weakness of batting. However, they shouldn't spend more time on their batting than their core strength of bowling. They should always spend the most time focusing on improving their strength.

I'd encourage leaders to better understand their individual strengths, and the strengths of their team members, and then work harder on improving these strengths than their weaknesses. A collective team complementing each other's weaknesses with their individual strengths brings just the right balance to make a winning team.

Author Tom Rath and leadership consultant Barry Conchie describe their findings in their book *Strengths-Based Leadership*. Mathews Johns Hopkins Medical Book Center explains,

> *Based on their discoveries, the book identifies three keys to being a more effective leader: knowing your strengths and investing in others' strengths, getting people with the right strengths on your team and understanding and meeting the four basic needs of those who look to you for leadership.*

The basic premises of the research are that people perform best when working in their strong areas and that teams perform best when the team itself has a balanced, complementary set of strengths. The data reveals that the most effective leaders are always investing in strengths. Employees who do not work in strengths areas are only nine percent engaged in their jobs versus seventy-four percent for people who do work in their strengths. Further, engagement has been proven to substantially increase productivity for the company. Focus on people's weaknesses, and they lose confidence. Focus on their strengths, and they are more confident, healthier, happier and wealthier over a lifetime.

Learning these building blocks will help you become a better leader. People always follow leaders. This is true for every microcosm of life, and every microcosm of our lives is ultimately a reflection of our leaders. The impact and influence leaders have on our lives and our world are limitless. Now, more than ever, we need *moral* leaders to impact and influence our world. You can be one of these leaders.

CHAPTER 7

TOMORROW'S LEADERS WILL CHANGE THE WORLD WITH THEIR HEARTS

Tomorrow's leaders will not lead dictating from the front, nor pushing from the back. They will lead from the center—from the heart."
—Rasheed Ogunlaru

Our understanding of leadership has changed over the last several decades. It would be safe to say that the way people expect leaders to lead has also changed. Dr. John Maxwell summarizes this well in *The Maxwell Leadership Bible*, where he outlines the four styles of leadership since 1950:

- "The Military Commander: Leaders came out of the army and expected unquestioning obedience from subordinates." (Many of our presidents had military backgrounds.)

- "The Chief Executive Officer: Most leaders migrated to a different style driven by vision and shared by everyone. Yet it was still top down and possibly very narrow in scope."

- "The Coach: Leaders moved toward a coach model where they saw employees as players on a team. This produced even better results but still limited the possibilities to the vision of the coach."

- "The Poet and Gardener: Today, leaders see the need to express the heart of the team, as a poet gives words to the hearts of readers. They develop players using encouragement and direction. They recognize the power of words and use them wisely."

Throughout **PILOT**, I've constantly reiterated that leadership is a heart issue. It's all about a leader's heart. It's my desire for tomorrow's leaders all over the world to begin developing their hearts. This is paramount! The single greatest attribute that tomorrow's leaders need in order to succeed is this: *They need to lead with their hearts.*

In this chapter, we'll deal with the final letters in the acronym **PILOT**, which are **OT** for **O**f **T**omorrow. We'll finish looking at building blocks that a leader of tomorrow needs to master and which will further complement the heart of a leader.

LEADING IN TOMORROW'S WORLD

Tomorrow's leaders face unique challenges. Our world is rapidly changing, so they'll require a specific set of skills to lead well. Following the Gallup study on strengths-based leadership, the Gallup research team also developed four domains of leadership strength:

1) Execution—making things happen
2) Influence—selling ideas inside and outside of the organization
3) Relationship building—being the glue that holds teams together
4) Strategic thinking—focusing on the big picture and the future

Fasttrack, a consulting organization, made the following observations during the "Rockefeller Habits" workshop, I attended several years ago, relating to current and future executive leaders:

■ Executives fail because of "bad execution."

■ The number one issue for future executives will be "finding and keeping talented people."

Let's review these leadership building blocks that both Gallup and Fastrack are predicting as necessary for tomorrow's leaders. But first, let's take a look at some of the challenges that leaders in the past have faced but look promising for tomorrow's leaders. Tomorrow's leaders will be dealing with the world as it appears to be getting better at an incredible rate. The real proof is in the data:

The Decline of Extreme Poverty

Nearly 1 billion people have been taken out of extreme poverty in 20 years. The world should aim to do the same again

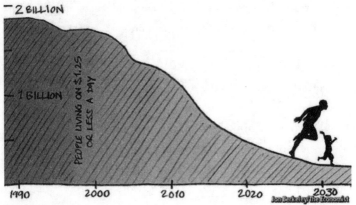

Source: *The Economist*

Entrepreneurial blogger Peter Diamandis in his post "Data . . . World Getting Better" states that "Absolute poverty is defined as living on less than $1.25 a day." According to *The Economist*, over the last thirty years, the share of the global population living in absolute poverty has declined from fifty-three percent to under seventeen percent. We've got a long way to go, but it is getting better. Over the next twenty years, leaders of tomorrow have the ability to extinguish absolute poverty. Think about that for a moment: as a future leader, you have the ability to extinguish poverty in the world.

Reduction in Infant Mortality Rates

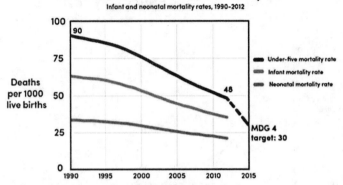

The Global Under-Five Mortality Rate
Infant and neonatal mortality rates, 1990-2012

Source: *Devpolicy, UN Interagency Group for Child Mortality Est.2013*

The chart above reflects the global infant mortality rates for children under the age of five between 1990 and 2012 based on the number of deaths per one thousand live births. In the last twenty-five years, under-five mortality rates have dropped by fifty percent. This rings true with another of Peter Diamandis's observations: "Infant mortality rates and neonatal mortality rates have also dropped significantly."

Education

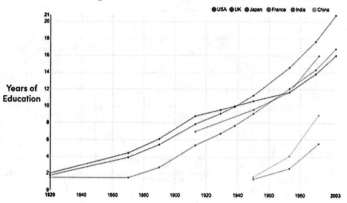

Source: *One World in Data, Max Roser*

While this chart excludes Africa, it still shows that in the last two hundred years, the average number of "years of education" received by people worldwide has increased dramatically. In the United States in 1820, the average person received less than two years of education. These days, it's closer to twenty-one years of education, which is a ten times improvement.

Worldwide Life Expectancy Growth

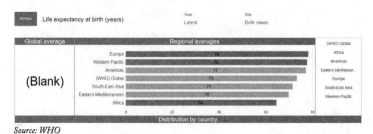

Source: WHO

According to the World Health Organization (WHO), global life expectancy has increased by more than six years between 2000 and 2019—from 66.8 years in 2000 to 73.4 years in 2019.

And based on data from John Snow Labs, the global average life expectancy increased by five "years between 2000 and 2015, the fastest increase since the 1960s. Those gains reverse declines during the 1990s when life expectancy fell in Africa because of the AIDS epidemic and in Eastern Europe following the collapse of the Soviet Union. The 2000-2015 increase was greatest in the WHO African Region where life expectancy increased by 9.4 years to 60 years," which was driven mainly by improvements in child survival, and expanded access to anti-retroviral medication for treatment of HIV.

Annual Hours Worked Per Person

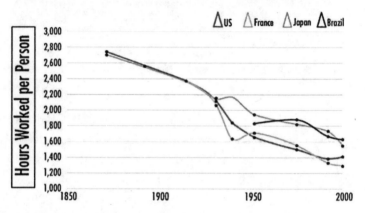

Source: Angus Maddison, The World Economy: A Millennial Perspective (Paris: OECD, 2001)

This chart shows that the annual hours worked per person has been steadily declining suggesting that people are taking a different approach to work and life as a whole.

Increase in Knowledge and the Pace of New Technology Adoption

Chart of the Week: The ever-accelerating rate of technology adoption

BY DREW DESILVER

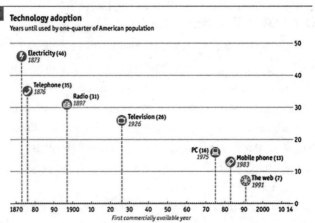

Technology adoption
Years until used by one-quarter of American population

Source: Singularity.com

The pace of technology and data will double. As reported at *Industry Tap*, technology writer David Russell Schilling asserted in 2013:

> *Buckminster Fuller created the "Knowledge Doubling Curve," as he noticed that until 1900 human knowledge doubled approximately every century. By the end of World War II, knowledge was doubling every twenty-five years. Today things are not as simple, as different types of knowledge have different rates of growth.*

For example, nanotechnology knowledge is doubling every two years and clinical knowledge every eighteen months. But on average, human knowledge is doubling every thirteen months. According to IBM, the build out of the "internet of things" will lead to the doubling of knowledge every twelve hours.

LEADERSHIP BUILDING BLOCKS FOR TOMORROW'S LEADERS

When you review some of the data trends, it's evident that tomorrow's leaders have the potential to redefine history in an unprecedented way. In 2020, the world experienced the COVID-19 global pandemic, and leaders across the world had to deal with extraordinary challenges that changed our world, maybe forever. But what if COVID-19 was just the trigger, and the real bullet will only happen once the virus is over? Will social distancing become permanent for our world to survive?

These nuances require a different type of leader with different skill sets, which will revolve around one key—having the "right" heart to lead. Let's look at several key additional leadership building blocks, which I believe tomorrow's leaders need to develop and be skilled in:

- Choosing your team
- Execution
- Leadership development
- Future thinking
- Conscious leadership
- Legacy

Choosing Your Team

One of the most important—many would say *the* most important—tasks of tomorrow's leaders is selecting and developing the right team. If an organization is struggling, but the team is functioning well, they have hope and feed off each other's encouragement. Jim Collins, in his book *Good to Great*, covered two principles when it comes to choosing your team: Get the right people on the bus, and once you get the right people on the bus, make sure they are in the right seats.

Right People on the Bus

Getting the right people on the bus (and the wrong people off the bus) is the first step in choosing your team. Jill Collins went on to say: "The main point of this concept is not just about assembling the right team—that's nothing new. The main point is to first get the right people on the bus (and the wrong people off the bus) before you figure out where to drive it."

Collins makes the point that some people want to get on the bus because of where it is going, but he suggests a better way:

Start with the right people on the bus, and then decide where to go. There is no substitute for getting the right people. It's a different hiring philosophy. Hiring the best people and letting them help decide the direction of the bus will always be better than hiring people who want to go where they think the bus is going. If the bus breaks down or changes course, the latter group wants off.

Future leaders must hire on attitude and train on skill. At his leadership institute, Dr. Chand advised we use the **ASK** model when choosing teams. The ASK model focuses on three attributes:

1) A—ATTITUDE

When we hire people with the right attitudes, we can teach them to do anything.

2) S—SKILLS

Dr. Chand stated, "We hire people for what they know and fire them for who they are." Their skills are the *what*. Their attitudes are the *who*.

3) K—KNOWLEDGE

Those with skill and knowledge can fix what is broken and explain why it broke in the first place.

Right Seats on the Bus

Once we have the right people on the bus, the next step is to ensure that your people are in the right seats on the bus. Why? Because proper people placement prevents problems (the 5 Ps in selecting a team). People are most productive when they're passionate about what they're doing. Always try to put people into positions they care about. I've used the 5Ps principle enough times in my career to know that it works and is a huge step in the right direction when choosing the right team.

Know Your Team.

Earlier I referred to a team I once adopted and how, in the first year of managing this team, I deliberately broke down the organizational structure to ensure each person in the team reported directly to me. I did this to get to know this new team well. While it proved tough to manage such a large team, the future benefits of me intimately knowing each individual member far outweighed the cost of my time.

To assist me in the process of getting to know my team, I adopted the 4 As model, which we also include in our **PILOT** program and could be beneficial to you. Use these four As to get to know your team better:

1) Attitudes—Dr Chand says, "This is who they are. Discover who they are by understanding their attitudes toward their jobs and the people around them."

2) Affinities—What do they like? Whom do they like? Dr. Chand continues, "Some team members may have an affinity for a previous leader. Knowing those alliances are still there can help current leaders" make a smooth transition.

3) Anxieties—What causes them stress? Who causes them stress?

4) Animosities—What is it and who is it they don't like?

Leaders can only respond to information if they know about it. Take time to get to know your players. Team members know who is performing and who is not. They also know who the toxic people are. They are always watching you, as the leader, and how you are handling these situations. In most instances, leaders are too afraid to deal with these issues because some of the toxic people might be the best performing people or the people with the biggest reputations, yet they have really bad attitudes. Replacing these people with encouraging and inspiring team members can help the entire organization function better.

I've faced this challenge many times in my life, and whenever I'm in this situation, where I know someone toxic in our team has to go, I use this. Charlie Crystle, co-founder of Chili!Soft said:

> *The number one thing you need to understand about building a company is that mediocre people drag down excellent people— they are a cancer and you need to cut them out as fast as possible. Don't worry about creating holes in the company—excellent people are much more productive when mediocre people are removed from their environment.*

Selecting Your Leaders

The most critical decision we make as leaders is selecting the leaders on our team. There are two characteristics found in people who work for us. They either think and act *like managers,* or they think and act *like leaders.* The biggest difference is that managers get the most out of themselves, but leaders get the most out of others.

In my numerous corporate roles, selecting my leadership team has always been the most important and yet most difficult task. It always takes me on a rollercoaster of emotions, frustrations and pain because I understand the importance of selecting the right leaders to have around me. The team you surround yourself with can either make you succeed or make you fail. For me, there was always a close correlation between my success and failure and the team I chose. During the constant deliberations and oftentimes confusion in selecting leaders, I applied another simple concept.

Dr. Chand's first book, *Who's Holding Your Ladder?* is a great read for any aspiring leader. The concept of "Who's holding your ladder?" will significantly impact the way you select your leaders. If the ladder is your vision, and you're the visionary leader climbing that ladder, you can only climb as high as the strength of the people holding your ladder—your ladder holders. The stronger the ladder holders, the higher a leader can climb in achieving his or her vision. The weaker the ladder holders, the more time a leader has to devote to keeping the ladder stable.

The following qualities should be key when selecting your ladder holders. Ladder holders must be:

- Strong: They can handle instruction and correction.
- Attentive: They pay attention and learn quickly.
- Faithful: They believe in their leader.
- Firm: Manipulative people cannot blow them about.
- Loyal: They don't question their leader's motivations just because they don't like his or her method.

These qualities are vital because the leaders you select will be holding your ladders. If they aren't quality people who are good at what they do, the ladder will never be stable, and it will impede your ability to climb towards reaching your vision. This is one of the reasons I get excited about our organization, LeaderGrow, as it helps to increase the organizational capacity or leadership potential for our clients because we help develop good ladder holders for them. Very few organizations have ladder holders who are readily qualified and trained because, in my experience, there are a lot of followers but very few real leaders. That's why it's important to mentor and develop the potential in future leaders. Make sure that the best people are on the bus and that the bus is pointed in the right direction. But, as leaders, we must be the drivers, and we need to control:

1) Who gets on our bus—We choose whom we want to be on our team.

2) Who needs to get off our bus—We decide to whom we need to say goodbye.

3) Where they sit—We select the places where our people are best suited.

EXECUTION

Tomorrow's leaders have to get both themselves and their teams to *execute* as this is critical in creating momentum to fulfill their visions. Execution (or the lack thereof) is one of the key reasons most executives are failing today.

> *After all is said and done, more is said than done.*
>
> —Aesop

Execution Is about Managing Expectations.

Remember that the definition of conflict is the difference between expectations and reality. As leaders, our job is to minimize the distance between expectations and reality. The best way to make sure that expectations and reality match is to communicate the details clearly and concretely.

Like me, I'm sure your diary is often overwhelmed with meetings. I often think that sometimes leaders misinterpret executing with having many meetings. Have you ever sat in meetings where issues get discussed repetitively, but no one is really doing anything about them? After these meetings, we think that we've fixed the problem, but we've just discussed the problem to death.

There is a simple solution for leaders to solve the execution problem during these meetings. Before moving from one agenda item to the next, answer the question, "Who does what by when?" If this question doesn't get answered, the job is not going to get done.

Execution Is about Inspection.

Dr. John Maxwell said, "People don't do what you expect; people do what you inspect."

Knowing who should do the task and when it's supposed to be done makes it easier for us to inspect and make sure that the correct person is being held accountable. Your job as the leader is to continue following up and tangibly inspecting that what was committed to be done has in fact been done.

Execution Disciplines

There are three execution disciplines that I learned while attending that "Rockefeller Habits" workshop a few years back:

1) Priorities—create alignment

2) Metrics/data—create clarity and foresight

3) Meeting rhythms—create better/faster decisions

Vilfredo Pareto said, "In any series of elements to be controlled, a selected small fraction, in terms of number of elements, always accounts for a large fraction in terms of effect." *4I.Design* states, "The Pareto principle (also known as the 80/20 rule, the law of the vital few or the principle of factor sparsity) states that, for many events, roughly eighty percent of the effects come from twenty percent of the causes." If you want the right outcomes most of the time, small disciplines help get you there.

Examples of how you could use these three execution disciplines in your organization are as follows:

1) Priorities

At the beginning of each year, set your key priorities. Have a minimum of two, but no more than five priorities for the year. For example, priorities include things like profitable growth, higher customer satisfaction, better employee engagement and improved quality. Finally test each of these priorities against your overall vision to ensure alignment. Priorities helps you create alignment.

2) Metrics

Include each of these priorities in a company scorecard with key metrics against them. For example, a revenue target, a profit target, a quality target and so on. This main scorecard is then agreed on and signed off by your entire team. You could take it further by getting each team member to break down the scorecard for their areas of responsibility and for their teams. For example, the sales team scorecard will include the revenue target and gross margin target, but may not include the profit target as this may not entirely be influenced by them.

The respective teams can use these departmental scorecards to execute against their targets. These scorecards provide your team and their respective teams clarity on what needs to be achieved and foresight as priorities can now be broken down by month and rolling year-to-date achievements. Remember: What you cannot measure, you cannot manage. Setting metrics helps create clarity and foresight, which will help you manage outcomes.

3) Meeting rhythms

Personally, I am pedantic about creating and keeping meeting rhythms because the bigger the amplitude of the wave, the more effective you become. For example, I typically set three meeting types to ensure our teams are executing against our priorities:

1) Weekly—These meetings are a temperature check against the month's targets. They are brief, structured meetings with quick decision making. They are nonnegotiable. Wherever you are, you will dial in for these meetings. They help me keep my finger on the pulse and they are core to me and the team executing for the month.

2) Monthly—These meetings are for a detailed review of the previous month's performance, reviewing our YTD performance and for strategic discussions.

3) Six-monthly—These are to test our half-year performance to ensure we are on track for the next six months and to ensure alignment against the priorities we have set ourselves for the year. These meetings are also more forward looking against our three-to-five-year strategic plans.

Dashboards are great tools to support the three steps in execution. Dashboards prevent you from being blindsided, help you to focus on the right things and allow you to spend more time solving problems.

Challenging Your Beliefs

Execution is about challenging your beliefs to create change for you and your team. When we talk about the three steps in execution, we often get the all too familiar comments:

1) "But you don't understand; our business is different."
2) "I don't have the time to do this. I'm too busy."
3) "Oh, no, another 'flavor of the month' process."

Key Reasons for Failure in Execution

- Lack of leadership or sponsorship for this process
- Focusing on too many "things"
- Not having clear, well-defined priorities, key performance indicators and weekly milestones
- Too "busy" to have daily, weekly, monthly and quarterly meetings
- Overcomplicating the process
- Culture with a lack of ownership and accountability and follow-through
- Leaders too busy working "in the company" vs. "on the company"
- Lack of willingness in the organization to change
- Lack of a clear vision

Tomorrow's leaders are going to require energy and speed to deliver on their visions, and the art of execution can contribute significantly to these visions being achieved.

LEADERSHIP DEVELOPMENT

The biblical account of Moses teaches us another important lesson as leaders: "You cannot handle it on your own" (Exodus 18:18, NIV). When Moses was the leader of the children of Israel leading them into the Promised Land, he played the role of CEO, COO, CFO, and HR. There was a time in his journey when he couldn't do it anymore; he was wearing himself out. That's when his father-in-law, Jethro, stepped in and suggested that Moses develop other leaders to help him in his journey. Something revolutionary happened after Jethro confronted Moses over his leadership methods. He went from doing to leading. Moses began to develop and empower other leaders.

Great leaders develop other leaders. Given the future challenges facing tomorrow's leaders, they need to be able to develop others around them. They will not be able to achieve their visions on their own. They will need strong ladder holders. There will need to be a process of multiplication versus addition. This process of multiplication can be translated as transformational leadership, which is the end goal for us when working with future leaders and organizations. When leaders make leaders, they know their work is done. Leadership development is about increasing the organizational capacity of your teams and organization by creating more leaders.

WHEN LEADERS MAKE LEADERS, THEY KNOW THEIR WORK IS DONE.

Balloons and Ceilings

In all organizations, there are balloons and ceilings:

- The balloons represent people who rise to a certain level and then stop.
- Leaders often function as ceilings, preventing the balloons from rising higher.

Leaders can raise the ceilings, and this is what we want to instill in the leaders of tomorrow. There is a school of thought in Africa that the only time the leadership changes is when the leader dies. It doesn't matter how that leader performs, they maintain this ceiling until death. It's almost similar to a marriage vow—I will stay in this position until death us do part. But what if we can raise our leadership ceiling and help everyone rise higher? That's what leadership development is all about.

Forbes recently did some research into "Which working benefits do millennials value most?"

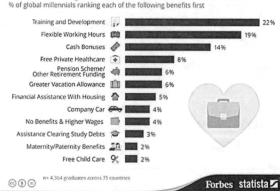

Which Working Benefits Do Millennials Value Most?
% of global millennials ranking each of the following benefits first

Benefit	%
Training and Development	22%
Flexible Working Hours	19%
Cash Bonuses	14%
Free Private Healthcare	8%
Pension Scheme/Other Retirement Funding	6%
Greater Vacation Allowance	6%
Financial Assistance With Housing	5%
Company Car	4%
No Benefits & Higher Wages	4%
Assistance Clearing Study Debts	3%
Maternity/Paternity Benefits	2%
Free Child Care	2%

n= 4,364 graduates across 75 countries

Forbes statista

Source: KPCK

The survey, originally conducted by PWC and recently republished in KPCB's *2015 Internet Trends Report*, reveals that most millennials actually consider training and development opportunities the most valuable working benefit, which is followed by "flexible working hours."

Further, my personal experience working with millennials is that they value company culture. In his article, "How Millennials Are Reshaping What's Important in Corporate Culture," Larry Alton agrees: "[M]illennials value company culture more than any other generation that's come before them. Even though the idea of "corporate culture" has been around since the 1970s, only recently has it started to become a bigger priority for workers." Tomorrow's leaders may have no option but to develop their people.

How Do We Raise the Best Leaders?

"There is a vast difference between training people and developing them," believes Dr. Sam Chand. "Training focuses on tasks; developing focuses on people." There are three ways of raising the best leaders in your team and organization.

- Do it yourself = too much work
- Hire it out = too much money
- Develop others = too much time

The third option is the least expensive, but it is also the riskiest. What if I develop these people and they leave? But as Zig Ziglar said, "The only thing worse than training employees and losing them is not training them and keeping them." In this regard, I applaud Deloitte. Deloitte adopted option three and poured themselves into developing their people. Being in a competitive business environment, the risk of these people leaving the organization was great, but that didn't stop them. Because of this, I'll always be a Deloittean at heart and an ambassador of this firm. I owe so much to Deloitte for developing me into the leader I am today. Deloitte was unconsciously developing more leaders, and even if these leaders, like me, did not always remain, they would still be leaders in society.

Raising Your Own Ceilings

Tomorrow's leaders must raise the ceilings for themselves as well. We need to remember that as we grow as leaders, we raise the ceilings of everyone around us. If I become a better leader, the entire organization rises with me. It is therefore important to always surround yourself with leaders who are better than you.

As a leader, do you have to be the smartest person in the room? I was taught, "If you are the leader, and you are the smartest person in the room, what a sad room that is." Why? Because you have stopped growing, and you have reached your ceiling. That's why it's so important to ensure you continue developing as well.

When executives reach a certain level of leadership, it is no longer about managing the product or service. It's about leading people. That is why great CEOs can easily transition from company to company because their talents aren't in products, they are in people.

Leadership is a matter of how to be, not how to do. This is the WHO and not the WHAT. When it comes to leadership development, your ultimate goal for the people under your watch is that they become better human beings, and that the ceilings get raised in their lives. When things are going right, use the "window" principle where you look through the window and praise the team. When things are going wrong, use the "mirror" principle where you look at yourself as the leader and take responsibility.

Just as the leader determines the ceiling for the employees, we determine the ceiling for the leaders who work for us. This balloon and ceiling illustration holds true at every level. If you become a better spouse, mother or father, then your family can go higher. So too, if your leaders can become better spouses, mothers, fathers and citizens, they can take everyone higher. This is transformational leadership at its best.

FUTURE THINKING

Tomorrow's leaders need to spend less time looking at the past and more time anticipating the future. Thinking about the future is fundamental to dealing with the challenges of today. You have seen that knowledge is multiplying at an incredible pace. People who graduated only a few years ago are now out of date. By ignoring tomorrow, we undermine today.

Figure 3: Source FastTrack

What do you see? In the top half of Figure 3, it shows a series of gadgets, and the bottom half has a single iPhone. I'm sure that some of the younger leaders reading this book are trying to figure out what some of the gadgets in the top half actually are. Only a few years ago, if you wanted:

- To listen to music—you needed a Walkman.
- To make a call—you needed a telephone.
- To record a video—you needed a video recorder.
- To tell the time—you needed a watch.
- To work—you needed a laptop.
- To take a photo—you needed a camera.
- To get a hold of someone urgently—you needed a pager.

Fast-forward ten to fifteen years later, and the only thing we need to perform all of the above tasks is one mobile phone. Wow! I tried explaining this to my kids, but they just didn't get it. The exponential growth in mobile phones has been nothing short of astronomical. When compared to personal computers (PCs), the smartphone industry dwarfs PCs with five billion people buying smartphones every two years versus just over 1.5 billion people buying PCs every five years.

Now take a look at Figure 4 below. Do you recognize some of these brands?

Figure 4: Source - FastTrack

In Figure 4, we see the new global brands. What is most interesting about these successful global brands is that:

- Uber is a taxi service—but it doesn't own a vehicle.
- Skype is a phone and video service—but it doesn't have any telephone infrastructure.
- Google is a research house—but it doesn't own any books.
- Amazon is a book store—but it doesn't have any stores.
- Airbnb is a hotel chain—but it doesn't have any hotels.

You get the point. On New Year's Eve in 2016, almost two million guests spent the night at Airbnb listings. It was a new record for a single night, and it is as many bookings as the two largest hotel chains have rooms. Most Fortune 500 companies take close to twenty years to reach a market capitalization of a US \$1 billion. Google, Facebook,

Uber and WhatsApp have done it in less than eight years. So, as leaders of tomorrow, "What are the questions we are not asking?" Or, are we asking enough questions in our organizations and on our teams?

If you also consider the current developments in 3D printing, stem cell development, driverless cars, advancements in healthcare and the new cryptocurrencies, you can certainly see why Mark Andreessen, founder of Netscape, was so right when he said, "Software will eat the world, in all sectors. Companies need to adapt or they will become extinct. In the future every company will become a software company."

FUTURE PLANNING

How do you go about planning for the future as a leader of tomorrow? Sometimes, we plan to have all the answers, but it's the questions we don't know. You need to create deliberate future planning incubators for you and your team to anticipate, innovate, read and experiment for the next three to five years for your business and industry. Let's take a closer look at these concepts:

Anticipate—You need to have teams focused on anticipating the "black swan" events that could create changes. A leader must anticipate change and position his or her organization to thrive in a new environment. You need to anticipate changes to your customer, your markets, your team and your culture. Wayne Gretzky said, "Skate to where the puck is going, not to where it has been."

Innovate—You need to have teams focused on innovating. The best leaders know that innovation must come from within workers and without. Leaders need to be asking enough questions.

Experiment—You need to have teams focused on experimenting. Most large organizations invest heavily in research and development centers to experiment on new solutions and offerings for their industries. As blogged by Peter Diamandis in his post "Raising Kids in Exponential Times," Jeff Bezos said, "The amount of useful invention you do is directly proportional to the number of experiments you can run per week, per month, per year. Following this line of thought, Bezos is also quoted in *Inc.com* columnist Jessica Stillman's article, "7 Jeff Bezos Quotes that Will Make You Rethink Success," "If you're going to increase the number of experiments, you're going to increase the number of failures." You'll also increase your number of successes!*Read*—You and your team need to commit to learning. Some of the world's greatest leaders dedicate themselves daily to exponential learning. Warren Buffett reads five hundred pages a day, Mark Cuban reads three hours a day and Bill Gates reads fifty books a year. Great leaders elect to read educational books and publications over entertaining literature. They are committed to continue learning.

To successfully implement the above, leaders may need to consider selecting internal and external resources. The long-term benefits of such a process will far outweigh the short-term costs. To be successful in the future, leaders of tomorrow need to have the muscles of a big company yet have the heart of a small company.

Remember, we may plan all the answers, but it's the questions we don't know.

Futuring Tomorrow's Leaders

Futurist and author Joel Barker observes that most leaders are not futurists, but they know that scanning environments and creating visions of the future will drive individual and organizational success. Leaders who have an eye on the future regularly forecast trends, envision scenarios and help to create the desired future.

"Futuring leaders" need to be vision-driven. They look through the windshield while they drive, not the rearview mirror. Their whole way of thinking and talking is focused on the future. The sad reality in most organizations is that leaders are in their comfort zones, so the leaders who got us to this point may not be the ones who carry us into the future.

YOUR COMFORT ZONE IS YOUR DANGER ZONE. —GREG PLITT

Greg Plitt, an American fitness model, actor and former Army Ranger, said, "Your comfort zone is your danger zone." Our new leaders will rarely be our old leaders. It's not that they're incapable of leading; it's just that they may be incapable of seeing the organization differently than when they came in. But we can't be futuring leaders alone. We must take time to help our teammates learn to be future gazers and future planners. We need to recruit future-thinking leaders to go with us. We need people who can envision the future. In his book *Futuring,* Dr. Chand aptly sums up future thinking when he relates the story of Walt Disney as follows:

> *After Walt Disney's death and the completion of Disney World, someone said, "Isn't it too bad that Walt Disney didn't live to see this!" Mike Vance, creative director of Disney Studios replied. "He did see it. That's why it's here." Vance understood how Disney envisioned the future. It was Walt Disney himself who said, "The future is not the result of choices among alternative paths offered in the present—it is a place that is created—created first in the mind and will; created next in activity."*

Conscious Leadership

Emotional Quotient (EQ) is a necessary building block in leadership, so much so that I have always focused on developing EQ more than IQ (Intelligence Quotient) in future leaders. In 1995, Daniel Goleman wrote his book *Emotional Intelligence—Why It Can Matter More Than IQ.* Since then, EQ is acknowledged and accepted as one of the key characteristics of great leaders globally. But businesses worldwide first accepted EQ suspiciously and still continue to delay its integration into their leadership programs.

During the COVID-19 pandemic, I came across an interesting article from entrepreneur Francesca Gabette who looked at IQ, EQ and a new term called the Human Quotient or HQ. She described how, during the pandemic, all IQ indices were not relevant and did not hold much value to handle the crisis. People worldwide were struggling to understand and explain the emotional and physical turmoil that they were experiencing. Even keeping hourly updates of the news, specialized reports or the many "flattening the curve" models were not helping people. For the first time in their lives, IQ believers were unable to find a convincing explanation for their followers. During that time, EQ became essential to survive and succeed. We experienced the best global EQ training ever.

The concept of EQ is attributed to Professors Peter Salovey and John Mayer. They stated that EQ is the "capability of individuals to recognize their own emotions and those of others, discern between different feelings and label them appropriately, use emotional information to guide thinking, decision making and behavior, and manage and/or adjust emotions to adapt to environments or achieve one's goal."

During the period of forced lockdown that many countries implemented to control the spread of the virus, we had to quickly learn the skill of not only understanding our own feelings, but also the feelings of others. Our fears were everybody else's fears. Empathy and emotional connections were keys for us to fight the virus. Managing our people and teams remotely meant that we needed to develop tools to listen to our people in real time. We had to learn how to build trust and alignment with our teams, while also making tough decisions, and all while we were social distancing. During the crisis, several leaders told me that they interacted more with their people then than at any other time before, and all of the interactions were digital.

Let's recap:

- IQ is not dominant anymore. Our rational minds need help.
- EQ is the true emerging force. It must be seen as an opportunity.
- A new concept, HQ, is meant to be the catalyzer.

Humanity is powerfully coming back to the center. Not betting on humans means to die as a society. Every technology, solution or service that we strengthen now using HQ will be more likely to survive and thrive in the future. Therefore, "conscious leadership" (EQ + HQ) will be required by tomorrow's leaders. EQ + HQ needs to be embraced now as the emerging future for tomorrow's leaders. The condition of the leader's heart will be key in mastering this "conscious leadership."

LEADERS OF TOMORROW NEED TO FINISH WELL

Leaders of tomorrow need to finish well. There is much to accomplish and much at stake, so we cannot fail. I'm convinced that leaders of tomorrow will not have the luxury of "messing up" and still expecting to finish well because they will have no place to hide given the global society we live in. We continue to witness leaders of today being exposed in their scandals. Once household names with great influence lose all their credibility in an instance of poor judgement. Since the turn of the century, large global brands such as Enron, Lehman Brothers, Arthur Anderson and WorldCom, have all been implicated in scandals and no longer exist. Where are the leaders of these companies now?

Earlier we discussed the dark side of leadership and how every leader must be wary of theirs. There is always the ONE thing—the one secret sin, the one weakness, the one thorn in the flesh—that is always fighting against a leader, preventing him or her from finishing well. Leader need to be aware of three things as they prepare for their leadership journeys that will help ensure they finish well:

1) Your secret sin will prevent you from finishing well.

King Asa is one of the many Old Testament kings in the Bible who started well but failed to finish well. Often, the pattern of failure stems from secret sin or a secret weakness in the leader's life.

Growing up in church and experiencing the pain and disappointment of watching many of my heroes not finish well, I wanted to finish well. Reviewing areas in my life, I realized that there were three common secret sins or weaknesses that could potentially derail leaders from finishing well. I summarized these three areas into the quirky acronym PMS—Power, Money and Sex.

There is always ONE thing leaders will struggle to let go of. I've identified my secret sin, and each day I come before God and hold myself accountable to ensure that it doesn't derail me. Don't get me wrong, I've made many mistakes and will no doubt continue to make mistakes. However, I'm succinctly aware that there will be consequences to my mistakes, and they could even prevent me from finishing well. I need to take full responsibility for that. When you mess up, (con)fess up!

WHEN YOU MESS UP, (CON)FESS UP!

During my tenure as CEO of Tip-offs Anonymous, we studied the profile of a fraudster to understand why people commit fraud. There were three elements to any person committing a fraud:

- Need—A person has a genuine need.
- Opportunity—A person sees an opportunity.
- Rationalization—A person rationalizes that what he or she is doing is not wrong.

For example, a single mom may require money in January to pay for her child's school fees. This is a genuine need. This single mom is also in charge of the petty cash box at the office. This is now an opportunity. She decides to take some money from the petty cash box and rationalizes to herself that she is not stealing. She is merely borrowing it until she gets her January paycheck, and then she will put the money back. Well, at the end of January, no one actually notices that any money is missing, so our single mom thinks it's okay to borrow a little bit more and more.

When we interviewed the biggest fraudsters, their stories were all the same. They started small and rationalized that what they were doing was not wrong. When nobody noticed, they continued. Over time, they became oblivious to the fact that they were actually doing something wrong. That's the biggest downfall of fallen leaders. They become immune to any reality and think that there is nothing wrong with their secret sin/s. They say, "Everyone else is doing it." Or they feel entitled to a little fun—until they get caught, that is. And if you ask, they will tell you that you will get caught one day.

Have you identified your secret sin? If so, what are you doing about it?

2) Sin in your camp will prevent you from finishing well.

There is another biblical story with a character named Achan. Achan was an Israelite who fought the battle of Jericho with God's servant, Joshua, the successor to Moses. God had commanded the Israelites to destroy the entire city of Jericho because of its great sin. Only Rahab and her household were to be spared because she had hidden the Israelite spies. God further commanded that, unlike most victories when soldiers were allowed to take the spoils, the Israelites were to take nothing from Jericho. The Israelites obeyed—except for Achan, who stole a beautiful robe and some gold and silver, which he hid in his tent.

Ultimately Achan's sin was discovered, of course. But more significantly, Achan's sin caused God's blessing upon the Israelites to be withheld in their subsequent battle against the city of Ai, and the Israelites suffered much loss in that battle. Thirty-six innocent men died because of Achan's sin. He stole that which was "devoted to destruction" and brought destruction on others.

Just as surely as fire burns, so to do wrongdoings have their consequences. Sin affects not only the one who sins, but others as well. Have you ever had a sore thumb after banging it with a hammer or the like? Didn't it hurt all over? You couldn't forget the pain—so much so that your whole body was affected. This is a good lesson for leaders of tomorrow. There are times when you cannot understand why things are going so wrong in your organization. Sometimes there are wrongdoings in your camp and you need to eradicate those persons or wrongdoings to ensure you finish well. There is an old proverb that says, "A little leaven leavens the whole lump." In your case, the malcontents may be few, but they will soon ruin the whole organization and derail you from finishing well.

3) Know your trigger points.

What do I mean by this? Know well the times when you are vulnerable to "messing up." There are many barriers you can use to ensure you don't mess up. I rely on two—(1) God—I'm accountable to Him and (2) Myself—I'm aware that messing up will prevent me from finishing well.

As a leader preparing to lead tomorrow, make sure your foundation is strong and that you lead with your heart. Tomorrow's leaders have a great task ahead of them, perhaps even more so than any other generation before them. Therefore, as leaders of tomorrow, make sure you start well. More importantly, make sure you finish well!

CHAPTER 8

LEADING A MEANINGFUL AND PURPOSEFUL LIFE AS A LEADER OF TOMORROW

The opportunity of a lifetime needs to be seized
during the lifetime of the opportunity.
—Leonard Ravenhill

f you picked up this book, then you probably have an innate desire to do something meaningful and purposeful in your life as a leader of tomorrow. I deliberately use the words *meaningful* and *purposeful* as I believe that this will allow a leader to focus their lives on serving others, rather than serving themselves. The late Bishop Eddie Long, the senior pastor of New Birth Missionary Baptist Church in Atlanta, taught me an important lesson when he said, "I am not afraid of failing. What I am afraid of is being successful in the wrong thing in my life."

This is what keeps me awake at night—the fear of failing to fulfill my God-given destiny of living the life that God has ordained for me. I always teach that the greatest amount of wasted potential is in the graveyard. Graveyards are filled with millions of people who had the potential to do something of meaning and purpose in their lives, yet they did not realize their potential. These people were "I wish I had" or "I should have done" people. My prayer is that you will not be one of them!

THE GREATEST AMOUNT OF WASTED POTENTIAL IS IN THE GRAVEYARD.

Throughout this book, I've covered many essential leadership traits that will help you become successful as a leader of tomorrow. But you also need to understand what your meaning and purpose as a leader will be, and they come from understanding your WHO as a leader. In this chapter, I want to take you a little deeper to help you find that ONE thing—your meaning and purpose—in your life as a leader of tomorrow.

FIND YOUR MEANING AND PURPOSE

Finding your meaning and purpose starts with finding your dream. A meaning and purpose isn't something you're entitled to. It's something that you earn, work for and strive for. You only deserve it if you go for it. I believe every single person has a meaning and purpose inside of them. But it's up to each individual to find their unique meaning and purpose—that ONE thing in their lives that will leave a lasting impact in this world.

During the famous Rivonia Trial, Nelson Mandela and the other accused activists were convicted of sabotage and sentenced to life in prison. "I Am Prepared to Die" is the name given to the three-hour speech given by Mandela on April 20, 1964, from the dock of the defendant. In the last part of this speech, Mandela poignantly said:

> *During my lifetime I have dedicated myself to this struggle of the African people. I have fought against white domination, and I have fought against black domination. I have cherished the ideal of a democratic and free society in which all persons live together in harmony and with equal opportunities. It is an ideal which I hope to live for and to achieve. But if needs be, it is an ideal for which I am prepared to die.*

Mandela found his meaning and purpose in life, and it was an ideal that he was willing to die for.

Wayde van Niekerk is a world record holder, world champion and Olympic champion in the 400 meters. At the time of this writing, he also holds the world's best time in the 300 meters. Born in Cape Town, van Niekerk is the only man in history who has run the 100m, 200m and 400m in under ten seconds, under twenty seconds and under forty-four seconds respectively. He has used his talent to inspire millions of ordinary South Africans.

Siya Kolisi, captain of the victorious Springbok team that won the 2019 Rugby World Cup, was the first black player to captain South Africa at test level. He did not have a privileged upbringing. Sarah Mockford in her article "South Africa Captain Siya Kolisi's Journey from Township to Test Star" for *Rugby World* reports:

He was raised by his paternal grandmother in a small township in Port Elizabeth. He often did not know if he would eat each day. He would go to school because he would get a meal but had to stop attending when he was ten to look after his sick grandmother who then died in his arms. Many of his friends fell into smoking and drinking. . . . He first tried [rugby] when he was seven. Most of his family played rugby, so it was natural that he would sign up for the local club in the township—African Bombers. Five years later, his talent was spotted, and he was offered a scholarship to Grey Junior School in PE and latterly the high school. He "didn't speak a word of English" when he first arrived but did manage a language exchange with one of his classmates, Nicholas Holton teaching him English and Kolisi teaching Holton Xhosa.

He went from being a young boy, who knew what it felt like to be poor and hungry, to a young man who inspired millions of young black children as South Africa's first black Springbok captain. When he led his team to victory in 2019, he united a nation.

These are just a few examples of ordinary South Africans who did extraordinary things. There are other examples of people who have inspired me along my journey to finding my meaning and purpose in life as a leader of tomorrow.

Stephen Hawking was one of the world's leading scientists. Jim Kelly reports in his article "Seven Things Stephen Hawking's Life Can Teach You About Running Your Own Business" posted on his *Wave Blog* that in 2006, Hawking asked: "In a world that is in chaos politically, socially and environmentally, how can the human race sustain another one hundred years?" He later added: "I don't know the answer. That is why I asked the question, to get people to think about it, and to be aware of the dangers we now face."

Hawking, however, according to "The Future of Perception: Brain-Computer Interfaces—Part 2" written by Philipp Markolin, "[Had] a rare early-onset, slow-progressing form of amyotrophic lateral sclerosis (ALS) that [had] gradually paralyzed him over the decades." And, at the end of his life, "he communicated using a single cheek muscle attached to a speech-generating device." Revered for his nonviolent philosophy of passive resistance, Mohandas Gandhi was known to his many followers as Mahatma, or "the great-souled one." He began his activism as an Indian immigrant in South Africa in the early 1900s. In the years following World War I, he became the leading figure in India's struggle to gain independence from Great Britain. Known for his ascetic lifestyle—often dressed only in a loincloth and shawl—and devout Hindu faith, Gandhi was imprisoned several times during his pursuit of non-cooperation and undertook a number of hunger strikes to protest the oppression of India's poorest classes, among other injustices. After the Partition of India of 1947, he continued to work toward peace between Hindus and Muslims. Gandhi was shot to death in Delhi in January 1948 by a Hindu fundamentalist. Gandhi's nonviolent acts of civil disobedience helped free India from British rule and inspired future generations of world leaders.

These are two more examples of ordinary people who found their meaning and purpose and did things in their lives that impacted the world they lived in. There is also meaning and purpose inside you—you've just got to believe it! How do you find this meaning and purpose in your life? It all begins with finding your DREAM. Here are five steps, coincidently using the word DREAM as an acronym, which will help you with this process of finding your meaning and purpose.

DREAM stands for:

D—Find your Dream.

R—Remove the "turkeys" from your life.

E—Embrace God.

A—Maintain a positive Attitude.

M—Believe that nothing is iMpossible.

Let's explore these five steps.

FIND YOUR DREAM

We all have dreams. Your meaning and purpose is found in living your dreams. God is also a BIG DREAMER. You are the creator of your dreams, big or small, and they have no limits. A dream is strong enough to define you. Once dreams are accomplished, you prove to others that they have no say in who you can and cannot be. Finding your dream is understanding the *possible* you.

If I were to give you a blank check and ask you to use it to fulfill your dream in life, what would you use this it for? What is this dream? What brings you the most joy and fulfilment in your life? What are you so passionate about that you lie in bed each night staring at your bedroom ceiling thinking about it? Finding your dream is the first step in finding your meaning and purpose as a leader.

What is your dream? Think about that for a minute. What does meaning and purpose mean to you? When you allow others to define your success, you discount the special gift that you've been given to bless the world with. Stop viewing success only in terms of the material things, but rather see success as the opportunity to fill a gap in the world—with meaning and purpose.

Remember the six stages in a dream taught by Jentezen Franklin:

- I thought it. . . . It just won't let go of you.
- I caught it. . . . Start talking to people about it.
- I bought it. . . . Pay the price and take a risk.
- I sought it. . . . Nobody can talk you out of it.
- I got it. . . . Grab hold of the whole prize—no regrets.
- I taught it. . . . There is no success without successors.

Using these six stages, let me take you through how my dream unfolded so that you can gain a practical application of this process.

I thought it.

I love helping people. I always knew I wanted to help people in some unique way. I also realized that the best and most fulfilling times in my life were when I was helping people by teaching them to become better in their lives—from one-on-one settings and teams of people in the office to congregations of people at church events. I felt like I was making a difference in their lives and doing something meaningful and purposeful in my life by impacting their lives. If you ask my wife, she would tell you that I can never stop talking when I am helping and teaching people. It just gives me the most intense feeling of joy and total satisfaction. I once helped a friend teach at his start-up home church. There were two adults and five children that Sunday morning, but that didn't matter to me. I just wanted to teach. After that church service, I thought to myself: *I just want to teach and help people become leaders.* I was so happy and fulfilled.

I caught it.

I started talking to everyone I knew about my dream. I remember those days of talking to others about helping and teaching people. They were the best days. I used to lie on my bed thinking about traveling the world helping and teaching people to become better people.

I bought it.

Then it happened! I remember it like it was yesterday. I watched Dr. Chand teach at a leadership event in a little suburb in Durban. That was the day when I truly bought into my dream. Watching him on that stage, I knew that was what I wanted to do for the rest of my life. It was during this season that I began paying the price and taking the risk in following my dreams. It was when I first began forming our leadership company.

I sought it.

Growing up in church, it was natural for me to become a pastor and lead a congregation the way my grandfather did and my dad does. As I began plotting the path to teaching leadership, no one could understand what I was trying to do. I had many detractors. Some of my closest friends didn't believe in what I was doing and thought I was just being silly. "You are called to be a pastor," everyone said. But this dream of teaching leadership and helping future leaders was now completely part of my DNA. No one could talk me out of it.

I got it, and I taught it.

I am now in these two stages of my dream. I'm in a phase of transitioning fully into my dream and grabbing the whole prize with no regrets. This book is part of my transition phase, which will launch me into the "I got it" and "I taught it" stages of the dream process.

Right now, I want you to get a piece of paper and write down your dream. It may take you days, weeks or even months, but don't stop until your dream becomes crystal clear to you. Don't let another day go by without starting to pursue your dream.

Finding your dream is the beginning to you finding your meaning and purpose as a leader of tomorrow. It's the most liberating feeling you'll ever have in your life.

REMOVE THE "TURKEYS" FROM YOUR LIFE

To lead a life of meaning and purpose, you need to be surrounded with people (leaders) also leading meaningful and purposeful lives because great leaders produce great leaders. If you want to fly with the eagles, then you need to remove the "turkeys" from your life. That is, you need to remove all the distractions. Most times, you can tell where people are going in their lives if you just take a look at the last ten people they spoke to on their phones—they indicate the company they keep.

TO LEAD A LIFE OF MEANING AND PURPOSE, YOU NEED TO BE SURROUNDED WITH PEOPLE (LEADERS) ALSO LEADING MEANINGFUL AND PURPOSEFUL LIVES BECAUSE GREAT LEADERS PRODUCE GREAT LEADERS.

Who are these turkeys? They are the bad influences and bad habits. Like those friends who are up to no good and always getting in trouble. Like those colleagues who have no plan and purpose for their lives. Like those people who add no value to your life, are always negative and constantly drain you more than uplift you. It's those bad habits or secret sins that keep holding you back from taking the final BIG step towards your dream.

Growing up, I made a conscious decision to cut the turkeys from my life. If you want to fly like an eagle, it takes discipline and hard work. Did you ever watch pythons killing prey? They kill their prey slowly by constriction and suffocation. When a python has you in its grip, each time you breathe the grip tightens. Some have said that, when a python has you in its grip, the only way to kill it is by cutting off its head. The distractions in your life are like pythons that slowly constrict and suffocate your dreams out of your life. Don't let these turkeys or pythons rob you of your life of meaning and purpose!

You need to surround yourself with eagles—leaders who are doing great things. Eagles are the chiefs over all the winged creatures. They are humankind's connection to the divine because they fly higher than any other bird. I learned from the *American Eagle Foundation* that the eagle with its keen eyes symbolize perspicacity, courage, strength and immortality, but is also considered "king of the skies" and "messenger of the highest gods." With these attributed qualities, the eagle became a symbol of power and strength in Ancient Rome. Eagles are among the largest and most powerful birds in the world. They are wise and careful to avoid danger. Eagles have been noted as symbols of strength, bravery and courage. You're sure to learn four things when you fly with great eagles (leaders) in your life:

1) You can never be in a comfort zone. Eagles have the longest life spans, but to reach this age they must make a hard decision. In its forties, its flexible talons can no longer grab prey, its sharp beak becomes bent and its heavy wings become stuck to its chest making it difficult to fly. The eagle is left with a choice: to die or to go through a painful process of change for 150 days. For us to get to our dreams and lead a life of meaning and purpose, we need to constantly change our way of life. Change is needed to survive, get rid of old memories, habits and past traditions and get free from past burdens.

2) "An eagle never eats dead meat," according to the Linkedin profile of Ms. Mirlande Chery. "A true leader spends time with people who are vibrant and liberal in thinking. You have to be with people who can think, make informed decisions and take

action. These are the people who bring change to society. They are lively, active people. Go out and look for them."

3) An eagle is not intimidated by its prey regardless of its size or strength. Eagles persevere to get to their dreams. No matter what the circumstances, you will learn to forge ahead towards your meaning and purpose.

4) An eagle flies into a storm and uses the force of the storm's winds to buoy it, so it can fly ever higher.

Who are the turkeys, or what are the distractions, in your life? Finding your dream and a life of meaning and purpose will require you to remove them.

EMBRACE GOD

To find your dream and significance, you need to find and embrace God. Why? You need to know that God created you for a purpose and a plan. When you don't know why something is made, you don't ask the creation, you ask the Creator Himself. You need to ask God, "Why did you create me?"

Your background doesn't determine God's plan for your life. Your dream can't be messed up by your circumstances. You need to stop making excuses for yourself. Excuses are the lies we tell ourselves to justify why we cannot live better. Excuses are the fortresses we build in our minds that engineer failure. What if the only thing that stood between you and your future were excuses? Jamelle Sanders said, "Dreams manifest at the intersection of excuses and expectations."

When you were created, God encoded you for an assignment and gave you the power to get it done. He placed meaning and purpose inside of you. King David said this of God: "You know me inside and out, you know every bone in my body; You know exactly how I was made, bit by bit, how I was sculpted from nothing into something" (Psalm 139:15, MSG).

Finding your meaning and purpose will mean finding and embracing God in your life.

MAINTAIN A POSITIVE ATTITUDE

Your attitude determines your altitude—this is a common phrase in the business world. In an earlier chapter, I mentioned that as a leader you hire people on attitude and train them on skill.

You *always* need to maintain the right attitude. If you have a positive attitude, then you are going to face life positively. We have too many people who aren't thinking about big dreams because they're around people who have negative attitudes. I refuse to have a negative attitude. There is nothing worse than a person with a bad attitude. If you have some of these people around you, then you need to get up and run as far away from them as you can. I am not advocating for leaders to be unrealistic, but I am asking leaders to keep moving forward.

Finding your meaning and purpose will mean *always* maintaining a positive attitude.

BELIEVE THAT NOTHING IS IMPOSSIBLE

The truth is that we all can do the impossible.

To live a life of meaning and purpose means that you will need to believe that you can do the iMpossible. Do you really want to do the impossible in your life? A person with BIG dreams is more powerful than a person with all the facts. The facts may be real, but the truth is greater than the facts. The truth is that we all can do the impossible. You must ask, "What is the art of the possible?" at every stage of your dream. As Mandela said, "It always seems impossible until it's done."

"8 Stories of People Who Proved That Nothing Is Impossible," published on *BrightSide* on June 3, 2016, tells the story of Nick Vujicic, an Australian who was born with no arms and legs:"I don't need arms and legs; I just need Him."This credo helped Nick to become one of the most famous motivational speakers, receive an economics degree, get married, and have two children. Nick Vujicic inherited his strong will from his mother. In one of his books, Nick told how her words set the tone for a lifetime. "Nicholas," she said, "you need to play with normal children because you are normal. You just have a few bits and pieces missing, that's all." Nick writes books, sings, surfs and plays golf. He often travels around the world with his lectures to help young people find a reason for living, and to realize and develop their abilities and talents.

The same article chronicles the life of Ray Charles recipient of twelve Grammy Awards:

As a child, he began losing his sight, and before the age of seven he went completely blind. When Ray was fifteen years old, his mother died. The young man couldn't sleep, eat or speak for many days. He was sure that he would go mad. When he got out of his depression, he realized that, having gone through this tragedy, he would be able to handle anything. When he was seventeen, the musician started to record his first soul, jazz and rhythm and blues singles. Nowadays, many people consider Ray Charles a legend. His works are even included in the Library of Congress. In 2004, after his death, Rolling Stone named Ray Charles number ten in the top one hundred greatest artists of all time.

I also often have to pinch myself, especially when I'm in the board-rooms of some of the largest companies in the world, sitting next to seasoned and highly qualified executives. How did this all happen? I believed and still believe in the iMpossible. Now, Kirbashnee and I have started our very own leadership consulting company. We've found our dream, and we're building towards a life of meaning and purpose by helping future leaders of tomorrow realize their dreams.

As a leader of tomorrow, I encourage you to use these five steps to help you find your dream, your meaning and purpose and those audacious goals in your life.

DREAM BIG AND LEAD WITH MEANING AND PURPOSE

My desire is that **PILOT** leaders will transcend the earthly measures of success and move into the heavenly measure of living their lives faithfully serving our Father in heaven with meaning and purpose. The tangible benefits of success often overshadow the intangible benefits of meaning and purpose. Many leaders will taste success in this world, but not many will taste meaning and purpose. For the few that do taste a meaningful and purposeful life, it will merely be the appetizer. The main course and dessert are especially reserved for them to taste beyond this world—when we meet the Father and His Son in His Glory.

Dream BIG, chase after your dream and go lead with meaning and purpose.

CONCLUSION

"Well done, good and faithful servant. . . ."
—Matthew 25:21 (NKJV)

When I started this journey of wanting to help develop future leaders, my motives were different from what they are now. I had this grand vision of making a significant impact in the world by reaching out to large audiences in packed venues, being a sought-after expert on leadership, and making lots of money. But I'm grateful for the process of maturing that has taken place inside of me over the years through the many experiences in my personal leadership journey. This book has been many years in the making, and purposely so, as I constantly challenged the integrity of my motives. I could certainly *talk the talk*, but could I *walk the walk* of what I was teaching future leaders? I'm humbled and grateful that this book has finally moved ahead. In this last chapter, I want to give you my personal summation of the foundational truths of genuine leadership.

IT IS NOT ABOUT YOU

If you are a genuine leader, then you will know it is not about you. It has never been about you, and it never will be. It is always about others—the people you are leading. Genuine leadership is about developing a heart to lead the people with whom you have been entrusted. Rassie Erasmus, the Springboks World Cup winning coach, once said, "True leadership is helping others to succeed." If you are making this about you and your success, then you need to test your motives. That's what I have done along my leadership journey.

LEADERSHIP IS SERVING

Genuine leadership is evident when leaders are there to serve others, not to be served by others. They lead from the front with humility by setting an example, they lead from behind in support, and they lead alongside in a mature and participative way. In the Bible, Jesus Christ gives us the perfect example of servant leadership. He said, ". . . The Son of Man did not come to be served, but to serve, and to give His life a ransom for many" (Matthew 20:29, NKJV). Even the Son of God came to serve others to the point of washing the feet of His disciples. You should also serve your people as their leader. Are people serving you, or are you serving your people?

LEADERSHIP IS ABOUT THE HEART

Throughout this book, I've made the point that leadership is a heart issue—it's all about a leader's heart. You will make many mistakes along your leadership journey, but as long as you keep the focus on developing your heart, then it will certainly work out well for you.

When you lead with your heart, you will always ensure that you do the right thing. Leadership is all about the heart—it's about having a heart for the people and a heart for the cause. What is the condition of your heart as a leader?

BE THE BEST YOU

Authenticity is a great virtue. But many a time, I've found the need to impress others and pretend to be someone I am not in order to be accepted. This weighed me down heavily for years because I was never content, never satisfied until I found the real me. I found who I am, and I am who I am by the grace of God. That's enough. There is no need to pretend to be someone else. Just be the best you as a leader. Finding the best you is the most liberating feeling in the world. It takes all the pressure off when you know that you can lead by just being you.

AS I SAID AT THE BEGINNING, THE WORLD IS A REFLECTION OF ITS LEADERS—BOTH GOOD AND BAD. IF YOU WANT TO CHANGE THE WORLD, THEN WORK ON CHANGING ITS LEADERS.

As a leader of tomorrow, what will your reflection show to this world? I am hopeful that helping to develop godly, integral and principle-centered leaders through **PILOT** will be mine. When my life is completed on this earth, and I go on to meet my LORD and Savior, Jesus Christ, I just want to hear the words, "Well done, good and faithful servant." My prayer for you is that you grow into a godly, integral and principle-centered leader and that someday you also hear those words.

God bless you on your leadership journey.

INSPIRE

INTRODUCING THE INSPIRE COLLECTIVE

While many churches are effective in equipping Christians for ministry within their walls, some struggle to prepare them for service in other arenas—their workplace, their neighborhood, their social community.

But the call to be change-makers is for all believers: Artists, business people, civic servants, community leaders, educators, mechanics, stay-at-home parents, students, and wait-staff.

That's why the Inspire Collective was established, to help raise up true influencers who are kingdom-focused Monday through Saturday, not just on Sundays.

The Inspire Collective delivers a unique blend of inspiration and application, spiritual and practical, for those wanting to impact and influence their everyday world for Christ.

THE INSPIRE COLLECTIVE OFFERS

- MAGAZINE
- BOOKS
- STUDY RESOURCES
- COURSES
- LIVE CLASSES
- EVENTS
- LOCAL NETWORKS

FOUNDED BY
Mike Kai, Martijn van Tilborgh, Sam Chand

COM